THE LANGUAGE OF HANDWRITING

[Page of handwritten signatures, rotated 90°. Visible names include:]

- Abraham Lincoln
- Victoria R
- Gladstone
- G. Fenimore Cooper
- Alexander von Humboldt (Hughes?)
- A. Dumas, fils
- Dumas
- Martinus Luther
- Bret Harte
- Lip. Washington
- Ellen Terry
- Wilkie Collins
- Rd. Baxter
- John Newman
- Thomas A. Edison
- W. Gladstone
- M. Osborn Shakespeare
- T. Hughes
- Pietro Paolo Rubens
- M. Bzentnel
- Thomas H. Huxley
- Charles Dickens
- Henry Irving

Thomas Hardy

J M W Turner

J S Mawson

Charles Darwin

Nathaniel Hawthorne   George Frideric Handel

Alexander de Humboldt

Ruskin

E Gibbon

Napoleon

R Browning

W Gladstone

Shelley

Peter Cooper

Longfellow

Wilhelm
J.R.

[*Frontispiece.*]

Copyright 1994 by Newcastle Publishing. Published by Newcastle Publishing Company, Inc., P.O. Box 7589, Van Nuys, California 91409. All rights reserved. No part of this book may be reproduced in any form without the express written consent of the publisher, except by a reviewer, who may quote brief passages in connection with a review.

ISBN: 0-87877-190-5
A Newcastle Classic
First printing 1994
10 9 8 7 6 5 4 3 2 1
Printed in the United States of America.

Originally published in 1901 by Brentano's Publishers, New York.
Cover design by Michele Lanci-Altomare

THE LANGUAGE OF HANDWRITING
A Textbook of Graphology

by Richard Dimsdale Stocker

author of
The Human Face, As Expressive of Character and Disposition
A Concordance of Graphology and Physiognomy
Physiognomy, Ancient and Modern

A Newcastle Classic

Newcastle Publishing
North Hollywood, California

"I have remarked a perfect analogy in the language, movement of the body of a person, and his handwriting. The more I compare different handwritings, the more am I convinced that handwriting is the expression of the character of him who writes. Of him whose figure is oblique, whose mouth is oblique, whose walk is oblique, whose *handwriting* is oblique—that is, in an unequal, irregular direction; of him the manner of thinking, character, and conduct are oblique, inconsistent, partial, sophistic, false, sly, crafty, whimsical, contradictory, coldly-sneering, devoid of sensibility."—LAVATER.

AUTHOR'S PREFACE

In commending this work to the consideration of that section of the reading public to whom it may appeal, I do so feeling that the subject with which it deals is one of the utmost importance and interest to all, especially those who have much correspondence to do.

Among those who have, in one way or another, borne actual testimony as to the utility of Graphology, or their belief in it, may be mentioned Goethe, Lord Beaconsfield, Nathaniel Hawthorne, J. C. Lavater, Edgar Allan Poe, Sir Walter Scott, Mrs. Elizabeth Barrett Browning, Lord Lytton, Wilberforce, and Archdeacon Whately; and, although it is not always the best plan to pin one's faith on the authority of "great names," I advise all, who have not through personal acquaintance with the subject, proved Graphology to be unreliable, to inquire into it and judge for themselves.

I lay particular stress upon this point, for the only course open to me in demonstrating the principles and worth of Graphology in the following pages has been to select the autographs of well-known personages for elucidation, and some people, who look at the book casually, will (very naturally) feel inclined to say, "Oh, it's easy enough to give talents to Sir Henry Irving or vices to Charles Peace." Yet had I given the writings of the *genus* "nobody," how could I have enlisted the sympathy of the public, much less shown the truth of the science, for obviously private people's writings (although they might possibly reveal talent of a high order) could not have had the same attraction for the world at large as those which I have selected.

Herein, then, lies the great necessity for personal knowledge; and, having insisted on this point, I will let the book speak for itself.

R. D. STOCKER.

N.B.—(When this or that celebrity's autograph is referred to, the signature in question can be seen, generally speaking, by securing a work[1] in which *facsimiles* are included; or else by visiting the MS. department of the British Museum.)

---

[1] For example—"Autographs and Birthdays of Eminent Persons" (Sampson Low), and the "Philosophy of Handwriting" (Chatto & Windus), which may be procured by the student of Graphology, and will be useful to him or her.

CONTENTS

	PAGE
I. Introductory Remarks to the Study of Graphology	1
II. The Materials Necessary for the Practice of Graphology	15
III. Constitution, including a few Words on the History of Handwriting	18
IV. The Handwriting Generally	25
V. The Finals and Commencements . . .	49
VI. The Letters considered generally, and the Characteristics disclosed by them . .	56
VII. The more Important Letters considered singly, and the Laws which Govern them . .	61
VIII. Flourishes	82
IX. The Forty-two Mental Faculties, with their Graphical Signs	87
X. Delineating	139
XI. Elementary Studies	143

CONTENTS

	PAGE
XII. ADVANCED STUDIES	160
XIII. ADDITIONAL STUDIES	239
XIV. HEALTH AND HANDWRITING	249
XV. HANDWRITING AND HEREDITY . . .	254
BIBLIOGRAPHY	258

THE LANGUAGE OF HANDWRITING

I.

INTRODUCTORY REMARKS TO THE STUDY OF GRAPHOLOGY

GRAPHOLOGY (from the Greek *grapho*, "to write," and *logos*, "a science"), which has been spelled sometimes *Graphiology*, or, as it has been written frequently, "Graphomancy" (from the Greek *grapho*, "to write," and *manteia*, "divination"), is the science and art which deals with handwriting as an index to character, &c.; the divination, in fact, of mental and physical peculiarities by the inspection of a person's penmanship.

Some writers have said that the subject is an *art* only; but that it can claim to rank as a science is proved, inasmuch as it is founded on elements and principles.

That some exponents of Graphology will apply its laws with greater precision, and deduce more correct

2 THE LANGUAGE OF HANDWRITING

conclusions than others, is true, for all mortals are fallible; and, as medical practitioners make mistakes, so may graphologists.

The science, however, is based on observation, research, and experiment; not speculation. Hence, if the rules which govern graphological analysis are properly applied, failure should be out of the question.

Although the subject is comparatively modern in the form in which we know it, it really dates back several centuries, and has been said to be "as old as the hills."

During the last twenty years it has become wonderfully popular, and deservedly so, for its value as a means of recognising the characters of those with whom we are corresponding cannot be over-estimated.

It may seem strange, at first sight, that none of the earliest volumes upon Graphology appears to have excited much attention, since occultism, for the most part, is merely a revival of what was at one time the rage with certain classes of the community.

But if we reflect for a moment, we shall remember that a few centuries or so ago comparatively few people could write, and those who did so wielded the pen in so laborious a fashion as to render their writing, not actually worthless, but, in some respects, unsatisfactory for the purpose of graphological analysis.

I have myself delineated the characters of an immense number of people from their writing during the past few years, and am in a position to testify, from personal experience, to the unfailing gratification which Graphology, when properly practised, affords to all sorts and conditions of men. All are interested to learn something about themselves, no matter whether they be high or low, rich or poor, learned or ignorant.

I have had my "experiences," which, however (unlike many of my contemporaries), I shall not inflict upon the reader,—as well as my "tests," which have invariably borne testimony as to the truth of the science.

Not only has Graphology received attention at the hands of those who are always ready to hail with fresh delight anything novel or strange, but it has excited the interest of learned as well as celebrated men and women; the late Mrs. E. B. Browning and Lord Beaconsfield being amongst that number.

Without doubt, the greatest writers upon Graphology have been, generally speaking, of French origin. But the oldest work extant, it is believed, is said to have been written by Baldo, an Italian, in 1622. It does not appear to have excited any great interest in the subject, however. The Abbé Flandrin of Paris, some thirty years since, systematised graphologic analysis, when the subject was raised above the level of mere intuitive guess-work, but it was not until the Abbé Michon, in 1872, published a work dealing with the matter, that Graphology really took a definite form. Although this was the case, it is only indirectly, nevertheless, that we owe an indebtedness to the Abbé Flandrin, for he himself left us no written exposition of his science behind him; and it is to one of his pupils, Jean Hippolyte (who, in collaboration with M. Desbarolles, the great authority on palmistry, produced an important work dealing with the subject), that the resuscitation of Graphology, in a popular sense, must be referred.

Miss Rosa Baughan, who was the first modern English writer to put her name to a work treating on Graphology, published, about 1875, some admirable papers on the subject, which have since formed the only important work in the tongue.

Desbarolles, in his works, connects Graphology with Chiromancy and Astrology, showing how the hand is influenced by the action of the planets upon it. But neither he nor any other subsequent writer, so far as I am aware, has shown the specific signs for each and every mental faculty, or attempted to trace the presence of this or that organ in the handwriting, by pointing out its exact graphic equivalents, as they are presented in the following pages by me. Indeed, hitherto no book on Graphology (with which I am acquainted) has given the signs for "Weight," "Size," "Time," "Tune," "Locality," "Eventuality," "Sublimity," "Constructiveness," "Hope," "Marvellousness," "Inhabitiveness," &c., as I have attempted to do.

INTRODUCTION

Many—nay, *most*—writers have confounded the qualities due to the organs of "Self-esteem" and "Approbativeness." By following the course of the present work, this confusion will be altogether avoided, and the matter rendered much easier of comprehension. It would have given me much gratification, had the course been a practicable one, to have acknowledged the source from whence this or that graphologic sign had its origin—by whom it was discovered and its history.

As, however, this mode of procedure would have been entirely out of the question, I have been compelled reluctantly to abandon the idea altogether.

As a rule, the various faculties localised in the handwriting have been found out by long-continued research. Hence, although a complete history of their discovery would have proved exceedingly interesting, and instructive even, to some of my readers, the method employed in each and every instance must have been similar, if not absolutely identical

Several traits described in the following chapters have been "located" (*i.e.* brought to light) by myself; and the novel way of arranging the graphical signs under the phrenological nomenclature cannot but prove more simple and comprehensive than any mere table of characteristics that I could have given.

There are *no exceptions whatever* to the laws of Nature. If we think we have discovered a sign—whether cranial, facial, graphologic, or otherwise matters little

6   THE LANGUAGE OF HANDWRITING

—to be representative of a particular characteristic, and then discover that such a one is met with apart from a person manifesting the trait, shall we say that our science is therefore only *partly reliable?* Certainly not; let us bravely confess that we have been on the wrong track altogether, and proceed to look elsewhere for data.

Before, however, we can justly confess ourselves outwitted, we shall do well to make out thoroughly the case which has apparently upset our calculations; for many people are in possession not only of characteristics which are in a latent or dormant state, but of faculties which actually work in such a manner as to deceive even those with whom they are on the most intimate terms.

Some people have "objected" to Graphology on the grounds that the style of writing is due merely to imitation. (See autograph of Mr. Clifford Harrison.)

But such an objection is ill-founded; for although a person may copy the writing of another—in which case he would *sink his own individuality for the time being*[1] —it is only that style which comes natural to one that is any test at all of character.

---

[1] It has been shown that, as handwriting is peculiarly adapted to indicate the mood of the writer, it will vary, *within certain limits,* when he is under the influence of any special feeling. It has been proved by experiment that it is almost impossible for any one to simulate any passion (either physiognomically or graphologically) and at the same time free himself from the feeling associated therewith. The reader is advised to test the truth of this.

INTRODUCTION

To prove that the style of handwriting is not *acquired* solely, I give the following statements of two of our most eminent medical men, Sir Samuel Wilks, Bart., and Dr. Henry Maudsley. The former writes to me: "The subject is one of great interest, and in which I half believe. Handwriting is hereditary; my brother's and my father's are very much alike." (September 22nd, 1897.) Again (July 11th, 1898), Sir Samuel says, in answer to a note of mine addressed to himself: "You have clearly shown how handwriting is hereditary. I have known this because I have seen many members of a family write alike, although *they have lived apart and been educated separately*." (The italics are my own.) He goes on to remark that, "Education must, however, introduce a fallacy; for some years ago all girls were made to write angular, scratchy letters, and now they are made to write round hand." Which fact, so far from upsetting our calculations, merely goes to prove the differences of character between now and then, the one generation being more prim and the other more easy-going—"New-womanish," as some have it. Sir Samuel Wilks adds, however: "Some time ago, when wanting a maid-servant, I was shown a letter in which not only were the letters well formed, but it was well expressed, and stops put in. All this must be taken into account when judging of a letter." To which I answer, "Yes; and much more besides!"

I might dwell further upon these statements and

8 THE LANGUAGE OF HANDWRITING

similar evidence which Sir S. Wilks has to offer; but enough has been said to show that even a learned physician is not above noticing the elements of Graphology.

Dr. Maudsley says in his communication to me: "There is one lesson which my handwriting teaches, namely, *that <u>Nature is stronger than art</u>, <u>heredity than acquisition</u>.*[1] When I was at school it was resolutely and systematically changed. But this conquest of culture (if conquest it was) has been gradually effaced, until now, in age, my handwriting has reverted to the stock form, and might almost be mistaken for that of my father. If my present handwriting then reveal character, it will be a revelation of the character of my forefathers." This note was written on August 11th, 1898.

Now some people, perhaps, cannot substantiate these statements. They, perhaps, do not think their writing sufficiently individualised either to be said to resemble that of the other members of their family, or even to be itself "twice alike."

This may be partly true.

<u>*Scientists*</u>, as we shall <u>see presently</u>, <u>write consistently because of the supremacy of *bone* in their organisations</u>, *which accounts for the testimony of Drs. Wilks and Maudsley;* and the general run of people are not scientific; hence the (alleged) variability of their style. But <u>although</u>, *at first sight*, <u>people's</u>

[1] The italics are again my own.

INTRODUCTION

<u>writing may appear different at different times</u>, it will not seem so if we *inspect it closely*.

Besides, we look at the shapes of the letters, the height and mode of dotting the *i*'s, the way in which the *t*'s are crossed, &c. &c., more than anything else; and if the writing of a person be said to "change" from time to time, let us but notice these and other like signs, and we shall soon find that there is no appreciable alteration in their "hand."

Objections such as this are puerile; but as "the proof of the pudding is in the eating," I subjoin a few (unsolicited) "testimonials" taken at random from among my letters, in order to show what the painstaking student may achieve.

Mr. WILSON BARRETT's business manager says:—
"Mr. Wilson Barrett desires me to say that he well remembers the sketch, which was very good."

Aug. 19, 1898.

Mr. MAX BEERBOHM writes:—"The opinion of my friends and relations is that you have shown great insight.—With kind regards, I am, yours very truly,

Feb. 8, 1899.   MAX BEERBOHM.'

Mr. FREDERIC HYMEN COWEN writes:—"I think the analysis of my signature is an excellent one, and as far as I can judge, correct in nearly all the particulars.—Yours very truly,

May 5, 1897.   FREDERIC H. COWEN."

10   THE LANGUAGE OF HANDWRITING

Miss (" LA LOÏE ") FULLER'S secretary writes thus:
—" Miss Fuller desires me to say that she read your sketch, and was very much pleased, as were several of her friends who read it."

Oct. 12, 1897.

Miss EVELYN MILLARD writes as follows:—" Please forgive my not having acknowledged sooner the delineation of my handwriting. I was delighted.— I remain, yours very truly,

Sept. 18, 1897.   EVELYN MILLARD."

Miss ALMA MURRAY (Mrs. FORMAN) writes:—" As far as I can judge my own character, I should think most of what you say my handwriting shows is true. —Yours very truly,   ALMA MURRAY."

Oct. 3, 1897.

Miss OLGA NETHERSOLE writes:—" I thank you for the reading of my character; it is most comforting in many respects, and true I think, at least I hope so.   OLGA NETHERSOLE."

Mar. 3, 1898.

The Rev. NEWMAN HALL, D.D., " Is quite willing that Mr. Stocker should print the character of himself—if he desires to do so—as it is considered to be a very good description of it by one qualified to judge.   H. M. M. HALL."

Nov. 22, 1898.

INTRODUCTION

Miss OLGA NETHERSOLE writes:—"Very many thanks for the very clever character sketch you made of me.—I sign myself, OLGA NETHERSOLE."
June 2, 1898.

"MAX O'RELL" says:—"I think the character sketch very good. It corresponds perfectly with the one Prof. Hubert drew some time ago (from the head).—Yours very truly, PAUL BLOUËT."
April 14, 1898.

Miss ALMA STANLEY writes:—"A very true delineation of my characteristics—at least, so I am told. With kind regards.—Believe me, sincerely yours, ALMA STANLEY."

The theory which, I think, places Graphology on at once the surest and simplest basis, is that which I now put forward:—*We think and act according to our formation.*

It stands to reason, therefore, that, when once we have mastered the inherent meanings of the various factors in *FORM*, we have the key to Graphology; and not only of that science, but of every other besides of a similar character.

Thus, we find that *rounded* persons produce *curvilinear* handwriting, because *they think* and *move* in *circles* and *curves;* whereas, *squared* and *angular* individuals, whose motions are *linear* and *angular*, trace *straight* and *rectilinear* characters. (Look at the handwritings of children and of the aged as extreme types of the above.)

The one belongs more especially to the "*infantile* stage" of life—the other partakes of the "*adult* phase" of existence.

The *fingers* of the former will be more tapering and better adapted to form the segments of a circle than those of the latter.

The softness of the bodily tissues, the relatively great malleability, the youthful elasticity and flexibility in the one case, and the hardness, firmness, stiffness, stability, and rigidity in the other, serve to account, broadly speaking, for the differences which are discernible in each instance.

The *curve*, having its highest manifestation in the human physiology in *round muscles*, which *curve* the extremities and *round out* the entire organism; and the *line*, having as its most perfect exponent *square bones*, which produce or create a series of straight-lined contours, at once prove the adaptability, versatility, and artistic proclivities of those of the muscular build, and the rectitude, morality, and scientific bias of those in whom the osseous materials preponderate.

These facts are self-evident, and since the whole physical or theoretical basis of Graphology may be satisfactorily traced thereunto, I do not propose to enter more fully into the rationale of the matter.

INTRODUCTION

The Esoterical side of Graphology I must leave severely alone, since any attempted explanation thereof, in default of there being any adequate means of tracing the course of connection, up to the present time, between the functions and organs of the viscera and senses of the cerebral structure, would end in disastrous failure.

I therefore appeal to the *common-sense* of my readers in submitting the signs given hereafter.

It seems to me to be only reasonable to suppose avaricious people would (as we find they do) cramp and pinch their writing by endeavouring to save every scrap of paper and every drop of ink they possibly can; that methodical persons should write carefully, minding their stops, crossing their *t's*, and dotting their *i's*; that practical, vigorous, well-sexed individuals should drive their pen with a will, employing a strong forcible movement in order to produce a strong, well-delineated "hand;" that hopeful folks should write an expansive, soaring style; that the cautious should pen a prudent "hand," and so forth.

It appears to me to be only logical to believe that (for example) *straightforward* persons would do things —move their hands, &c.—in a direct, straight-away, upright, downright fashion.

We have only to extend this to the act of writing, and, even as the trail of the slimy snail shows us the course it has taken, so the *recorded* pen-gestures register the character.

In truth, it may be said <u>we write not merely with our fingers, but with our *brains*</u>.

<u>Internal rather than external causes occasion the writing to take whatever shape and form it does</u>; hence, such changes even as the choice of an uncongenial pen will bring about will not *absolutely* destroy the normal indications of character, for the minor variations due to such are, after all, of no more account or consequence to the graphologist than are the effects of the ever-varying emotions which pass across the face to the physiognomist.

When all is " said and done," mere theories as such go for very little—are next to nothing, in fact.

Personal observation is the great thing, and those who are interested in Graphology have but to study the subject carefully for themselves in order to test it, and by so doing become convinced of either its truth or the reverse.

II.

THE MATERIALS NECESSARY FOR THE PRACTICE OF GRAPHOLOGY

THE *Requisite Data.*—A *bonâ-fide* sample of the subject's writing, comprising, *if possible*, a couple of pages or so of MS. (consisting of, at least, a dozen lines of handwriting), together with two or three directed envelopes. The following conditions are those under which it is necessary that the specimen should be written:—

(*a*) In an *absolutely* natural, unstudied, and spontaneous manner (because an artificial or a disguised mode of writing obscures the personality of the writer, in just the same way as would an assumed facial expression or mask);

(*b*) In *ink*,[1] which should not be "muddy," nor blotted with dirty blotting-paper;

(*c*) With the writer's *favourite* nib (a *split* one, not

---

[1] It will be well if the writing fluid used be of black or blue-black shade. This might be insisted upon by the delineator, as, although red or violet ink will answer the purpose almost equally well, the brightness of such colours is very apt to try the eyes, and hence render the graphological signs confused,

16 THE LANGUAGE OF HANDWRITING

a " stylographic " pen), which should be in good condition;

(*d*) And upon *un*ruled and preferably *white* paper, which should not be of too poor or common a quality, neither of such a glazed character as to allow of the ink running;

(*e*) Together with a sample of the writer's signature attached thereto;

(*f*) And a statement of sex,[1] where the signature fails to reveal this particular. (This is *not a sine qua non*, but it is one of the conditions necessary when the analysis is given, as is customary, and in every way advisable, in the third person.)

It is, perhaps, scarcely necessary to append the two following rules; but in order that the *exact conditions* essential to successful work be known, they are subjoined.

(*g*) All specimens considered should have been penned under normal conditions, when in the writer's habitual spirits and usual state of health, not when tired, or under the influence of illness, narcotics, drink, extreme haste, or any very strong passion.

(*h*) And *under no pretext whatever* should *copied* matter be deemed admissible, as, when the thoughts

---

[1] Beginners imagine that to determine the writer's sex is quite an elementary matter, but such is not the case. Men and women both possess precisely the same faculties, modified by development.

N.B.—At the same time, the *composition* or *subject-matter* of any sample should be disregarded by the graphologist when judging **character.**

are turned away from the *act of writing*, the chirography is likely to lose its individuality, and hence be inadequate for the purpose of diagnosing character.

The would-be graphologist should also provide himself with a magnifying or reading-glass with a powerful lens, in order that he may examine the manuscript submitted to him closely. Not unfrequently critically dissecting the writing by this means brings to light much that would otherwise escape notice, for such graphic signs as the form of the dot of the *i* require very minute investigation in order to obtain anything like satisfactory results when delineating.

In inspecting the handwriting in suspected cases of forgery, the expert would probably rely chiefly upon such (apparently) slender data in order to draw his inferences.[1]

Last, but not least by any means, the student will require a bottle of ink, a pen or pencil and paper, him (or her) self, so that the impressions of the character revealed may be noted down.

Thus equipped, nothing remains to be acquired but a thorough knowledge of the laws of Graphology; this, it is hoped, will be gained by careful perusal of the following pages *plus* conscientious study.

---

[1] The specimen of handwriting should contain, if possible, *several examples* of *all* the letters of the alphabet, as well as plenty of capitals and a few figures.

III.

CONSTITUTION, INCLUDING A FEW WORDS ON THE HISTORY OF HANDWRITING

IT is *absolutely necessary* that, in order to understand our precise position, when we study Graphology, we should know something of the physical and mental "organism" of mankind; for without doing so we can know little or nothing why it is that written gesture is expressive of temperament. It is useless to try, as some writers have done, to dissociate handwriting from the temperamental constitution of an individual, because, to begin with, the characters of the penmanship, although dependent mainly upon the *nervous* condition of the writer, will partake of his *physical form* as well.

It is nonsense to pretend that a person can free him or herself from the temperament or organic structure peculiar to him or her, for, as far as can at present be judged, the physical is but the materialisation of the mental, which in turn is nothing but the manifestation of the spiritual. (This, it must be distinctly understood by readers of this volume, is the writer's opinion.)

CONSTITUTION 19

It is unreasonable to believe otherwise than that thought *has form*. If, therefore, this is so, we start with the assumption that the exterior body will be an exact (visible) replica of the (invisible) interior "spirit." Spiritualists entirely do away with the popular fallacy that "ghosts," *i.e.*, disembodied spirits, are shapeless masses of vapour, or that they are gaseous airy "nothings." They assert that they appear to one (so far as they have investigated) under precisely similar aspects as they did when in this body of clay; in short, that they are in nowise different from what they were when in the flesh. I give this paragraph for what it may be worth, as I am no spiritualist, and therefore unable to pass judgment on any phenomena pertaining to the matter at issue. What I wish to draw attention to is the fact that *form* is preserved outside this body of ours; that, in fact, the nerve-fibres, bones, muscles, cartilages, &c., derive their shape from *within*, and that they are moulded by *internal* forces, of the precise nature of which, it must be owned, we are sadly ignorant.

The Vital—"Vegetative," "Abdominal," "Arterial," "Thoracic," "Sanguine," "Lymphatic," "Phlegmatic," or "Nutritive"—system. This includes the organs of life-force and nutrition, enclosed within the abdomen and thorax, the intestines, liver, lungs, and heart. When prominently developed, the chest will be wide and deep, showing good breathing powers and vigour of the heart action; the abdomen being full

20 THE LANGUAGE OF HANDWRITING

and rounded, and the extremities plump and tapering. The physical "build," as a whole, accompanying this form is wide and deep, the shoulders broad and expansive, the neck short and full, and the head and face as a whole *oval*[1] or *rounded*.[1] The complexion, hair, and eyes will vary from *light* to *dark*, according to the dominance of the lungs, liver, &c.

The *keynote* to this temperamental form is *Feeling*.

The Handwriting of the Vital System.

A *circularity* or *curvilinearity* of the strokes; and not merely in the lines which form the base of the letters or those which precede the up or down strokes, but in such as take (normally) a vertical or lateral direction; a *slope* either to the right or left; freedom; fluency; expansiveness; eagerness; regularity; extension of the terminals; ascendant style; outlines traced with a definite, firm, steady (and sometimes heavy) pressure upon the pen; letters, &c., tending to be large as a rule; relative width between characters; return-strokes, flourishes, loops, and down-strokes bold and heavy; tails and loops long.

The Motive—" Muscular," " Mechanical," " Osseous," " Melancholic," " Bilious," " Choleric "—system. This includes the bony structure, together with the fibres, tendons, and sinews—the " locomotive apparatus."

[1] This will depend a good deal upon the form of the underlying muscular tissues, whether they be long, thin, and flat, or short and round.

CONSTITUTION 21

The special feature of this system is length of limb and height of body. The face, which will be either oblong or square shaped, will exhibit well-marked bony ridges under the eyebrows, wide cheek-bones, a ridged nose, a prominent chin, and deep, strongly defined jaws.

The complexion may be either *dark* or *fair;* but, if *strongly* defined, the system will be found associated with blackish hair and eyes, and a swarthy, or by no means fresh-coloured, skin.

The *keynote* to this temperamental system is *Will.*

The Handwriting of the Motive System.

Rectilinear or *angular* contour of strokes; contraction of writing; letters, &c., narrow; "a," &c., closed at the top; short up-and-down strokes; style, vertical, or nearly so; forcible, bold "hand;" finals left unfinished; matters of detail neglected; terminals shortened.

The Mental—" Nervous," " Cephalic," " Brain," " Cerebro-spinal," " Nervo-mental "—system, comprises the brain—the cerebrum and cerebellum—the seat of sensation, perception, consciousness, motion, and volition.

With a predominance of this system will be found a slim, finely-moulded figure, with a relatively large cranium—that is to say, a head particularly developed forward of and above the ears.

The nerves will be keenly sensitive, and the whole organism will be remarkable more for *sharpness* of outline than anything else.

Again, the colouring of the skin, hair, and eyes will depend upon circumstances; but they will be usually light, the first being soft and clear, the second fine and glossy, and the third bright and lustrous.

The *keynote* to this temperamental system is *Thought* and *Sense*.

The Handwriting of the Nervo-Mental System.

Sharpness, rapidity of utterance, and *vivacity of expression*—leading features.

Letters placed capriciously, in various directions, and, for the most part, close together and small; sharp, pointed characters; irregularity of alignment; lively-looking style; fluent "hand;" up-strokes (relatively) long.

It is scarcely necessary to point out not only that the afore-mentioned systems are seldom found greatly in excess, but that time and experience will bring about changes in the subject's temperament; for careful study of the section devoted to the consideration of the basic principles of form will render the matter self-evident.

Hence, although *heredity* will give a sub-dominance at times of the motive or mental systems, the *normal* temperamental constitution prevalent in childhood and infancy is the *Vital*, since the object in life of those of tender years is to eat, live, and sleep, like a vegetable—a purely chemical existence. External influences, as well as natural growth, serve to retard or promote certain phases of temperament; therefore, as the various stages and combinations of these —which inherited tendencies, surrounding influences, personal habits, mental agencies and conditions, or what not, will have wrought through the period of existence—are almost infinite, all that can be done in a work of this kind is to draw attention to the fact.

We do understand, to a very great extent, what may be termed the physical basis on which our theories rest, but we are baulked to no inconsiderable extent owing to the fact that we are unable (up to the time that this is being written) to trace the connection between this or that manifestation of character (in the face or hand, for example) with the cranial "centre" from which it is supposed to emanate.

In short, we cannot associate the nervous distribution with any degree of certainty with the manifestations of the various mental faculties.

Anatomists are busy every day localising centres of ideation, but up to the present their researches cannot be said to prove useful in any high degree to the psychologist.

It is perfectly true that *demonstrable scientific discoveries* assist the student of human nature, and it will be found that the more natural history, geology, botany, &c., be studied, the greater knowledge shall we possess of mankind.

The universe is one harmonious whole, and mankind is an epitome of all.

This being so, it stands to reason that the better we understand his complex nature, the more enlightened shall we become in other branches of learning and departments of science.

IV.

THE HANDWRITING GENERALLY

HAVING before one a satisfactory specimen of handwriting, the first things which present themselves to one's notice are :—(1) the style considered as a whole; (2) its position as regards the paper ; (3) the size of the letters; (4) their shape ; (5) slope ; and (6) the "texture" or consistency of the strokes of which they are composed.

These points we will take under separate headings, and, first of all, consider

VARIOUS STYLES OF HANDWRITING.

In order that we may obtain a thorough and practical knowledge of Graphology, it will, of course, be absolutely necessary that we should analyse the several strokes of the letters in the abstract, as it were. But so as to be familiar with the more ordinary *types* of handwriting which one meets, it will be well first to consider the most commonly seen styles as a whole.

I. *The Large and Bold Style* indicates broadmindedness, liberality, high aspirations, firmness, decision of purpose, openness, pride, magnanimity, frankness, resolution, independence, daring, courage, boldness, and a generally forgiving disposition. People who write in this manner are usually more manly and strong, self-reliant, and tolerant than either penetrating, observant, critical, or delicate minded. They usually possess, for the most part, an absence of ostentation, whilst their philanthropy, patience, spirit, force, resolution, and love of enterprise are well defined.

II. *The Small and Cramped Style* denotes a nervous, timid, reserved, hesitating, fearful, and short-sighted yet shrewd, argumentative, practical, economical, opinionated, critical, and more or less melancholy, disposition. Persons whose handwriting is of this class will not have much self-command or ardour, and are likely to display either physical or mental weakness, if not both. They will be of a conservative, plodding turn of mind, and their character will be petty and pinched-up. A shy yet reckless, irritable, non-progressive, unhopeful nature is also predicated from this type of handwriting. This style is essentially that of persons who are of the strumous diathesis.

III. *The Formal and Precise Style* indicates a methodical, ingenuous, practical, matter-of-fact, careful, calculating, and precise disposition. The individual who writes thus will be fond of ceremony and matters of detail. The faculties of order, constructiveness, and veneration, which contribute towards exactitude and conventionality will be more prominent than ideality. Commonplaceness, egotism, self-sufficiency, and positiveness of spirit, rather than either taste, imagination, warmth, or sensibility, will characterise the personality. The disposition of the individual who writes in this manner will be a platonic one, and there will be a love of affairs and official matters, passivity and narrowness of ideas, rather than romance of feeling or poetry of sentiment.

IV. *The Ornate Style.*—Ornamental writing denotes conceit, vanity, swagger, boastfulness, ostentation, egotism, imagination, appreciation, and perception of beauty in form, constructive ability, dexterity, and artistic talents, as well as a scheming, planning, light-hearted, buoyant, enterprising, adventurous individuality. People who write in this fashion usually possess a small reflective intellect, but they are generally active both in body and mind, and are seldom idle, although they are frequently occupied without results, beginning many things and finishing few. They possess a greater amount of energy than persistence, and have more hopefulness than foresight. As a general rule, persons who indite a style similar to the above are coquettish, insignificant, and vulgar-minded.

V. *The Plain and Legible Style* signifies sureness (if slowness), calmness, gentleness, carefulness, clearness, steadfastness, prudence, sagacity, and a predominance of the reflective faculties. People who write thus are generally serious, strong-minded, stable, and reliable, and they usually direct their gifts well and profitably; they labour with industry, take pains with what they do, and are useful rather than showy or ornamental.

VI. *The Dashing Illegible Style.*—This class of handwriting indicates a lively, exuberant, impatient, ambitious, and turbulent nature, as well as vividness of imagination and inspiration, more than ordinary intelligence, and sometimes a spice of genius. This type of handwriting also signifies violence of temper, and people who adopt this style are incapable of brooking restraint or contradiction, although they are of a forgiving nature, and possess down at bottom a kindly disposition. The character of people who write after this fashion is enthusiastic, fervid, down-right, charitable, and devoted in matters of affection; they are hot in controversy, but put their whole heart and soul into whatever they undertake.

VII. *The Regular and Fine Style* indicates that the organs of constructiveness, form, order, and ideality are dominant, and denotes that there is a deficiency of both imagination and originality. Executiveness, conscientiousness, industry, and energy will characterise the personality, and there will be a calm, cool, equable temper, common-sense, self-control, patience, neatness, good taste, consistency, exactitude, and accuracy. The taste of the individual who writes thus will be of an elevated or spiritual description.

VIII. *The Unsightly and Irregular Style.*—In this case the writer will be unevenly balanced, and there will be a want of harmony in the action of the faculties; the subject will be inattentive, abstracted, or indecisive; wanting in ballast, unsteady, slovenly, capricious, awkward, careless, unpractical, and quite unable to be depended upon. Constructiveness, which gives versatility, will be usually well defined.

IX. *The Rounded and Measured Style.*—The dominant faculties which are indicated by this type of caligraphy are:—Constructiveness and order. The tastes denoted are mechanical; strength, deliberation, clearness of conception, good judgment, coolness, steadiness, thoughtfulness, and a practical, patient, and resolute character being exhibited. Calmness, tenderness, sympathy, affection, and the æsthetic sense are also shown by this style, whilst the natural inclination will be towards ease and pleasure.

X. *The Pointed and Angular Style.*—With this method of writing the faculties of order, constructiveness, ideality, courage, and self-esteem will be amongst the largest; and consequently the disposition denoted will be vigorous, independent, self-reliant, impatient of restraint, and distinctly combative. Ambition, hopefulness, energy, sensibility, natural talent, force of character, will-power, marked individuality, and plotting ability, as well as wilfulness, acuteness, refinement, vivacity, gentility, penetration, tenacity of opinion, and quickness of temper, in conjunction with some selfishness and power of sarcasm, also, will be among the chief characteristics of the writer.

The foregoing ten styles constitute the chief ones which the graphologist comes across; they are seen, generally speaking, blended—seldom pure.

The Style of the Handwriting. — Quickly-traced handwriting, which is to be recognised by the absence of effort apparent in using the pen, in the easy manner of forming the letters (in the shortest way possible), points to mental activity, and consequently a high quality of organisation, rapidity of thought, and ease in the mental processes.

Slow handwriting, the strokes of which have been formed by a movement of the hand which is the reverse of rapid, denotes a slow intelligence and a want of readiness of perception, or embarrassment, and a want of activity, mental or manual, as the accompanying facts will determine.

Temperate, well-controlled handwriting indicates self-government, moderation, discretion, reflection, prudence, non-excitability, judicious reserve, cautiousness, dignity, mistrust, want of confidence, sharpsightedness, modesty, precision, calmness, timidity, or even dissimulation—in varying degrees, according to the accompanying *particular* graphic signs.

Very calm handwriting will indicate excessive indolence, inertia, and placidity.

Handwriting which contains a pronounced movement, and is irregular if not ill-regulated, shows impressionability, imagination, vivacity, spontaneity, impulse, impatience, ardour, animation, energy, enthusiasm, gaiety, variability of mood, gracefulness, inattention, susceptibility of temperament, communicativeness, usually a want of judgment, and sometimes insanity. As a rule, this type of writing shows a not inconsiderable amount of pride, as well as indecision, versatility, and caprice.

Tremulous handwriting indicates paralytic tendencies. The less complicated and more direct the strokes of the handwriting the more exact will be the writer's mind, and the more sincere, fair, and simple his or her character; whilst the greater the complication and entanglement of the lines, the greater the want of precision, mentally, and the more artificial, morally, will he or she prove.

Clear handwriting—distinctness of the strokes, the absence of "blind loops," "tails" or "heads," &c.—tells of lucidity of thought, clearness of comprehension. Confused, muddled writing, on the contrary, bespeaks a disordered mind, a clouded intellect, ambiguity of thought and the lack of clearness of conception.

Those whose writing is formed of clearly-cut, sharply-defined lines express themselves in a comprehensible manner, there is no mistaking their meaning or misinterpreting their import; whilst such as pen a confused, perplexed "hand" will be found invariably difficult to be understood and wanting in mental perspicuity, coherence, and so forth.

If the strokes be not only *regular*, but *all carefully delineated* and perfectly formed, they indicate attentive habits and accuracy; if the characters be cramped and hurried over, here and there one or two being omitted altogether, they would indicate a want of method, absence of caution, thoughtlessness, absent-mindedness, carelessness, and a temperament averse from waiting for wished-for results. When the characters are formed as though for a stencil-plate (*i.e.* the strokes being broken up), they denote absent-mindedness or anxiety.

The Position of the Writing upon the Paper.

When a regular margin is kept upon the left side, it shows æsthetic tastes, orderliness, a love of harmony and proportion.

If the writing is set so that an even margin is visible on the right side of it as well, it shows artistic perception, delicacy of feeling, and patience.

Should the writing be irregular, so that *no* margin at all is left between it and the edge of the paper, it shows a want of taste, economical tendencies—a decided preference for the *useful* as opposed to the ornamental; as a rule, vulgarity, also.

If the writing *ascends*, it shows a progressive, enter-

HANDWRITING GENERALLY

prising, ambitious, energetic, ardent, good-humoured, active, hopeful, cheerful, mirth-loving, and (often) persevering, strong-willed, and courageous personality.

People sometimes, I believe, write aslant on the paper "for the sake of effect." It would seem to the uninitiated that this mode of writing proved the exception to the above rule; but, as a matter of fact, it does nothing of the sort. It simply expresses their *vanity*—for all ascendant writing shows a desire to appear to the best advantage—if not actually to "show off."

Descending handwriting, that is to say, such as runs downwards at the termini of the lines, shows sadness, discontent, despondency, unhappiness, melancholia, a want of enthusiasm, and of self-reliance also; as well as physical weakness, ill-health, fatigue, debility, timidity, solicitude, discouragement, and indolence. It is said, as well, to denote a tendency to apoplexy, and *always* a weak, rather than a strong-minded nature.

At times, one comes across a specimen of handwriting which, whilst commencing with the free, up-mounting movement, gradually lapses into the down-drooping class. Here comes a conflict of judgment. This is said to denote "struggle in life;" and most assuredly indicates that the writer is suffering from embarrassment, and is endeavouring to combat his "unlucky" destiny.

As a matter of fact, this movement of the writing

is due solely to nervous conditions, and merely indicates " fatality" in the sense in which unenterprising, unbusinesslike people are deemed unfortunate.

When the writing is observed to maintain a horizontal position, that is, taking neither an upward nor a downward march, it shows good sense, calmness, moderation, generally sound health, straightforwardness, determination, and a medium degree of enthusiasm.

If the letters are squeezed together, so that the spaces between them are narrow, it shows an ungracious disposition, ill-nature, and a churlish, unsociable, reticent, and economical personality.

The letters, by being well spaced out and separated, though not necessarily on that account *unconnected*, indicate a friendly, kindly, easily-accessible, generous disposition; whereas people who write in the former manner often live the life of hermits and go without "creature comforts," those who write in the latter way are fond of enjoyment and pleasure, and believe in making not only themselves, but others feel at home and comfortable.

When the writing is spread out, wide spaces occurring between the words and lines, we shall find the writer extravagant, improvident, fond of display, comfort, and ease, and of a disorderly rather than a methodical nature. Usually this kind of handwriting indicates also lucidity of thought. Writing that is compressed, and the letters of which are crowded together, shows a matter-of-fact, economical, reserved, and somewhat argumentative personality.

The Size of the Writing.—Large handwriting shows, generally speaking, pride, high aspirations, generosity, large-heartedness, imagination, frankness, simplicity of nature, and boldness, though very often it is adopted by persons whose intelligence is of a slow order, and who are far-sighted and inclined to exaggerate; yet, as most mental states bear an intimate connection with physical states, this far-sightedness is usually accompanied by a sort of mental presbyopia, which I generally read as "sublimity," the faculty that gives breadth of range to the mental horizon, and predisposes one to deal with things as a whole, in an extended manner.

People who write big "hands" are fond of generalising, and rarely trouble themselves about details, which they call "useless" and "unnecessary complications."

Small handwriting shows economy, opiniativeness, but notwithstanding acuteness; also narrow-mindedness, reserve, a "microscopic" mind, bigotry, and usually pettiness.

Persons who write thus are, as a general rule, short-sighted, and disposed to look at matters in a very limited way. They are often "spiritually" inclined, and frequently cheerful. Mental subtlety, continuity of ideas, and power of absorption, one generally finds developed highly in conjunction with this mode of writing.

Whereas people who write large are satisfied with a conception of the whole of things, those who write small are fond of minutiæ, and love finicking work, of whatever kind their brain developments predispose them to follow or become interested in.

In point of dimensions, handwriting that is neither too large nor too small is the *best*, since it indicates a *balance* between the "love of the ensemble" and "regard for detail." In such a "fist," there will be indicated sufficient capacity for delicate, fine work and finish, and no little susceptibility, yet not overmuch care for minutiæ, even if the writer be not easily satisfied. As a rule, people who write thus are not contentious, hypercritical, or argumentative, as is the case with those who write a liliputian "hand."

When the letters are of *unequal* heights, relatively speaking, it shows versatility, also mobility of feeling, mental plasticity, sensitiveness, along with a certain amount of inconsistency, indecision, hesitancy, weakness, and sometimes untruth, if there be confirmatory signs of the failing.

Sometimes the size of the writing of a person will not only vary from time to time, but also be dependent upon the dimensions of the paper upon which he or she happens to be writing.

In that case it will indicate adaptability, mental flexibility, and usually, I think, imitative ability of some sort.

The Shape of the Letters.—All writing may be said to

Types.

Globose . 1

oval . 2

Linear. 3

Square. 4

Angular. 5

[*Face p.* 37

HANDWRITING GENERALLY

resolve itself into either (*a*) " round," (*b*) " curved," (*c*) " linear," (*d*) " square," or (*e*) " angular hand."

As to which of these forms will predominate will depend upon the subject's organisation (as entered into in the previous section). Even the element of the " point," however, " the least element of form," is represented by the stops and dots. (The meaning of the " point " is said to be the starting-point of growth and the *commencement* of the germinating process in the animal kingdom.)

Globular or Spherical Handwriting which, when seen pure, takes the shape of " round " or " text " hand, " copperplate," or " copybook " writing, and is what is taught to children (although many older people pen similarly), shows undevelopment, immaturity of mind, and an infantile state of being.

As a rule, persons who write thus are wanting in individuality—they belong to a class of what may be termed " mediocrities "—who love conventionalities, official matters, and generally move and think in a narrow groove.

Generally speaking, there is a childlike simplicity about people of this grade.

Curvilinear handwriting (that which contains oval letters, &c.) indicates artistic perception, and goes with an easy-going, peaceable, affectionate, calm, gentle, sympathetic, good-natured, kind-hearted, complacent, and imaginative disposition.

I generally find, in addition to the above, that,

when the bases of the "bodies," &c., of the letters are very wide, this kind of writing shows much "credenciveness," receptivity of mind, belief in hearsay, and a tendency to take things "on trust."

In *excess*, this type of writing usually accompanies an indolent if steady-going nature, and those who pen after this fashion are incapable of forming very decided opinions; they will indulge in sentiment and fancies rather than facts.

In "Handwriting and Expression," Mr. Holt Schooling states that handwriting which is composed exclusively of curves is "never very graceful;" but this is merely a matter of taste. Had he pursued his investigations upon the basis here set forth, he would have come to the conclusion (as I have done) that the more perfectly curved the style, the better cultivated and developed the æsthetic sense of the writer will be. Consequently we find the writings of Gustave Doré, Hans von Bülow, Handel, Meyerbeer, Longfellow, Grieg, F. J. E. Got, B. C. Coquelin, and many other persons celebrated in the world of art, constructed after a curved principle.

When the up and down strokes of the letters exhibit a tendency to *round in* or *out*—that is, to take a bowed form—I am led to believe that they show *musical capacity*—"taste" or "talent," as the case may be, according to the accompanying signs. To my knowledge this sign has not been pointed out by any one writer heretofore, many having previously

HANDWRITING GENERALLY

stated that right-handed, slanting, curved writing shows the faculty, which, however, is not the fact.

Taking numerous examples, I may mention that the curve of the sides of the letters is to be seen prominently in the "hands" of such eminent composers as Sir Arthur Seymour Sullivan, Felix Mendelssohn Bartholdy, Auber, Hans von Bülow, Sigismund Thalberg, Sir Michael Costa, Giacomo Meyerbeer, C. W. von Glück, Frederic Hymen Cowen, Giuseppe Verdi, and F. F. Chopin, amongst numerous others; and in those of such vocalists or executants as the following:—Jenny Lind (Goldschmidt), Therese Tietjens, Madame Albani (Gye), and Madame Patti, whilst the handwriting of the well-known singer, Jean B. Faure, slopes *backwards!*

Generally speaking, there is a peculiar *softness*, a kind of spreading, sprawling, undefinable motion about musicians' handwriting, which, as a rule, is quite *recognisable*. The student is advised to examine the signatures of Franz J. Haydn, Rossini, Paganini, Offenbach, Salvator Rosa, Grieg, Ignaz Moscheles, Weber, Wagner, Sir H. R. Bishop, Giulia Grisi, Luigi Cherubini, Bellini, and M. W. Balfe as examples, in order to acquaint him or herself with typical musicians' "scrawls."

Many orators, such as John B. Gough, Patrick Henry, Henry Clay, George Canning, and Richard Lalor Sheil for instance, exhibit great rotundity, some almost sphericity, in the forms of the outlines of their "styles."

Linear, or, as it has been called, "bar-like" writing, which is composed of a series of more or less perpendicular and horizontal strokes, shows firmness, steadfastness of purpose, regular habits, method, inflexibility, and, not infrequently, severity.

Rectilinear handwriting also shows power of sustained effort, love of work, obstinacy, and an arbitrary nature.

Square-shaped handwriting, which is always formed of course by means of the straight line, signifies a high state of mental development; hence intellectual, moral, and physical *greatness* and perfection, along with such qualifications as trueness, straightforwardness, "squareness," and usually *talent* of a pronounced description. An excellent example of this type is seen in the handwriting of Thomas Alva Edison.

Angular handwriting. The inherent meaning of the *angle* is regularity, trueness, and precision, also limitation, "law," and principle.

When the angle is *misplaced* or *exaggerated*, so that the bases of the letters are pointed, we find an abnormal or morbid condition, along with such qualities as practicability (of an extreme kind), quickness of temper, obstinacy, contrariness perseverance, hardness, sarcasm, penetration, selfishness, positivism, energy, restlessness, inquisitiveness, ambition a go-ahead nature, and, of course, a very incredulous, inconvincible turn of mind.

HANDWRITING GENERALLY

Spiritual force is said to be shown by very pointed writing. When the *t*-bar terminates in an *acute hook*, it indicates conjugality, faithfulness in the matrimonial relation, connubial love. The reason for this will be obvious if the nature of the *angle* be borne in mind. Very frequently angular writing pertains to peculiar, if not eccentric persons.

The *point* (which, as has been shown, signifies "motion," "germination," "progress") is represented in the handwriting in the dots, stops, &c., the specific meaning of which will be considered in their proper connection.

Thus far and no further are we enabled to trace the analogy existent between the form of the human organism and that of the writing in relation to the basic principles of Form, as, much against my own inclination, but perforce, I am compelled to forego elucidating the signification of the *cube* graphically. This form signifies "integrity," "wholeness," and "completeness," belonging, as it does, to the *adult* stage of evolution. The reason why I cannot enter upon the significance of this geometrical figure more fully is, of course, for the simple reason that a flat sheet of paper on which writing is traced cannot exhibit three plane surfaces.

It is, perhaps, almost unnecessary to explain that the *circular* and *linear* elements, which create Form, and to which it is practically, if analysed, restricted, are respectively exemplified (when the writing is of a

42 THE LANGUAGE OF HANDWRITING

normal character), in (*a*) the bases and tops of the letters, and (*b*) the up-and-down strokes, as well as in dashes, hyphens, bars, &c.

The standard to go upon may be approximately judged of by referring to a copy-book, though it should be borne in mind that, as a rule, the characters therein, being representative of writing as an *art*, are of an extremely curvilinear character. As the segment of a circle is the form of movement described by those in whom the *muscular* system is dominant, it will be found, from what has been already stated in connection with the basic laws of Form, that artistic tastes or talents, oratorical, dramatic, or musical ability, will be possessed by such persons; and, as the motions of those in whom the *osseous* system is the stronger are of a more linear character and bounded by *line* and *rule*, it will be equally manifest that mechanical or scientific powers will be displayed by the subjects.

Abnormal handwriting, such as is composed of either slanting, crooked, imperfectly curved, oblique, or bizarre pen movements, the lines of which it is composed being neither truly curvilinear, rectilinear, angular, nor rectangular, shows a defectively organised individuality, either mentally or physically, if not both. The precise indications afforded by the *law of imperfect curvation* (including obliquity, eccentricity, *perversion* of form and motion, as in left-handedness, &c., tending to produce awkward

HANDWRITING GENERALLY 43

or inapt movements of the hand) may be translated thus :—

[1] Obliquity = One-sidedness, immorality.
[2] Eccentricity = Non-stability, oddness, genius *or* madness, contrariness of thought and action, marked individuality.
[3] Imperfect curvation = Sophistry, knavery, defective functions.

The Slope of the Handwriting.—In like proportion to the inclination forward, to the right, of the handwriting, will be the writer's sensibility, interestedness, impressibility to external influences, power of loving, tenderness, and devotion.

Very often when this "slope" of the handwriting is present *in a marked degree*, the subject will be highly susceptible in temper, passionate, demonstrative, desirous of approval, and therefore liable to jealousy.

In excess, this class of writing shows a morbid, hypersensitive nature, very loving and lovable, but entirely governed by feeling (though much will depend upon the accessory or accompanying signs).

Upright writing, the strokes of which are vertical,

---

[1] Shown, for example, in the upslanting *t*-bar, also in irregularity of alignment, &c.

[2] Exemplified in extraordinary and unconventional shapes of characters.

[3] Exhibited by defectively constructed letters, signs, &c., as in filiformed characters.

shows coldness, an absence of quick, spontaneous sympathy.

People who write in this manner never suffer their heart to run away with their head; they are governed by "reason" rather than by "feeling;" are self-contained; evince considerable controlling force over their "softer" emotions; and are very liable to be misjudged in consequence. They can usually display a good deal of sarcasm, though their satire probably arises not so much from a desire to be caustic, as a certain disinterestedness which causes them to be more or less impartial in their judgments and unswayed by personal feelings in a matter. Writers of this class are generally determined, and often obstinate.

To mention a host of celebrities who wrote as above would not be difficult. Here are a few:—W. M. Thackeray, George Cruikshank, Thos. Carlyle, Douglas Jerrold, Oliver Cromwell, Dr. Samuel Johnson, Thomas Alva Edison, Mary Queen of England, and Elizabeth.

"Back-handed" writing, *i.e.*, writing that inclines to the left, I regard as an abnormal variety, it being accomplished by an awkward, inapt movement of the hand, and partaking, to some extent, of the nature of an oblique gesture.

It shows a mistrustful, diffident, suspicious, apathetic, often indolent, always brusque, frequently untruthful, and generally affected personality.

As a rule, I think, those who pen this sort of

HANDWRITING GENERALLY

"hand" are afraid of "giving the show away," of making themselves "too cheap," &c., &c.

This reversed slant, more often than not, accompanies an exalted state of mind and restrained emotions, and one writer (Mrs. John White), in a small primer upon the subject of Graphology, gives it as her opinion that people who write thus are impulsive and undependable.

Henrik Ibsen, the dramatist, and Mr. G. Bernard Shaw, the critic, both write after this fashion,

Very often, in fact more often perhaps than not, the letters slant in no *single* direction. In order to determine the amount of *feeling* possessed by the writer, however, in such a case, the *predominant movement* must be observed. If the letters are sometimes inclined and sometimes upright, it signifies impressibility, variability of mood, mobility of feeling, or, at any rate, agitation (if of an only temporary description), or caprice, indecision, or an unsettled state of mind.

Persons who write after this manner will be as changeable as the weather, as mutable as the wind, and as unstable as water.

Although I recognise the value of this graphological sign, when the various characters slant consistently *any one* way, I generally find that there is a full or large development of what—for want of a more comprehensive word—we term the faculty of "weight."

This gives control over the muscular system, and aids in dancing, running machinery, comprehending the laws of gravity and motion, of force and resistance, and so forth.

When inflamed with drink, or otherwise impaired, the function causes the writing to become agitated and irregular—testifying as to the disordered state of the subject's "nerves," also indicating exhaustion, fear, or alcoholic excitement.

Among those who particularly, either directly or indirectly, owe their indebtedness to a large organ of "weight" in the exercise of their various professions, one may name the dancer, the skater, the mechanist, the mechanic, the engineer, the billiard-player, the cricketer, the juggler, the conjurer, the pianist, the painter—in all of whom delicacy of "touch" and steadiness of limb are an absolute necessity.

The Thickness of the Handwriting.—To a great extent this will depend upon the thickness of the nib used; and as the choice of the pen is of itself indicative of character, this is a most important point for consideration.

A fine-pointed hard pen, such as is made of steel, will, unless great force be employed, produce thinner strokes than a broad-pointed " J " or quill pen.

Active, sharp, vivacious, quick-tempered, kindly, sensitive, refined, and affectionate people will select the former; whilst those who are self-willed, pleasure-

Examples, *illustrative of — organic quality*:

low.	high.

activity
strong.   weak.

Activity.   activity.

Excitability:
intense.   feeble.

Excitability   Excitability.

HANDWRITING GENERALLY

loving, and more steady or easy-going, will choose the latter variety.

One or two writers on Graphology have said that energy is shown by the preference for the fine pen, and a want of the attribute by the employment of the wide nib. This I do not believe to be the case. Granted that the person who uses the former will be the quicker and more "spry;" but he who drives the latter will have more latent force, even should he not possess the promptness for action.

Light, fine writing shows a delicate mind, as well as æsthetic tastes, elevation of thought, and purity of feeling, as a rule, and feebleness rather than strength or vigour of organisation; though *sometimes*, to be sure, a morbid, unhealthy nature, and moral, as well as physical, weakness. As a rule, however, those who write thus are spiritually inclined.

Thick, muddy, hairy-looking writing, especially if the down-strokes are not clearly cut and their edges are not sharply defined, shows sensuality, in some form or other.

With persons whose minds are mediocre, or of a common or low order, the tendencies would be towards bestiality, and a heavy, dense, and materialistic nature would consequently be revealed.

Generally speaking, people whose writing is of this type are liable to give way to excesses—to self-indulgence and gluttony.

If, as is very often the case, the writing does not

present a uniform thickness throughout, but comprises strokes and stops which are here and there dark and heavy, it shows more especially that phase of voluptuousness which has been not inaptly described as "sensuousness." People who adopt this method of writing are strongly moved by any form of beauty which appeals to the five senses; and are hence given to admire lovely faces and beautiful forms, delicious odours, soft, silky materials, rich-coloured fabrics, plaintive melodies, and tasty meats and drinks. This goes to show that there is a vast deal of difference between a gourmet and a gourmand. More often than not, those artists who are great colourists—such as Rubens, the late Lord Leighton, &c.—show the foregoing development in their handwriting.

Handwriting that is of a medium thickness throughout, upon the whole, gives the most favourable indications; for then the writer will possess moderately intense passions—will be, in fact, warm, but not consumed by his or her merely animal spirit; hence, providing that all else is equal, well-disciplined in respect to the amatory and kindred propensities.

V.

THE FINALS AND COMMENCEMENTS

THERE are several *general rules*—which are applicable to *all* letters, in a greater or less degree—which it will be well to bear in view at the outset of our study. I refer to the methods of *beginning* and *finishing off* the letters—in short, to their "Commencements" and "Terminals."

The making of a "tick," or up-stroke, at the commencement of any of the letters, is said to indicate quickness of temper.

When the letters commence with a *hook*—an inward-curved line—they show desire for acquisition, love of possessions, and usually egoism.

If, before actually forming the letters, a curvilinear and rapidly delineated line is observed, it indicates a powerful sense of humour—love of the ludicrous, buoyancy, and mirthful spirits.

A straight, inflexible stroke which commences the letters shows a love of contest—a quarrelsome, contentious nature.

The *finals* are more important. If curtailed and short, such would indicate a prudent, careful, reticent nature; also, when seen in a "hand" bearing unmistakable evidence of mistrust, they would show, further, excessive calculation, solicitude, and extreme forethought in the character.

Long, extended terminals denote vivid powers of fancy, as well as liberality and generosity. It is not a difficult matter by any means to determine from the length of the final strokes of the characters the degree of extravagance or thrift the writer possesses.

All altruistic personages, among whom one can name the Baroness Burdett-Coutts, John Howard, Mrs. Elizabeth Fry, the Earl of Shaftesbury, the Earl and Lady Aberdeen, and Miss Florence Nightingale, write or wrote in such a manner that the finals are flowing and outstretched to the right. Close-fisted people pen a style in which all the terminals stop short and appear amputated or docked.

Well rounded-off and raised finals bespeak benevolence, also graciousness of manner and courteousness of bearing.

When the terminations of such letters as *d* are thrown back to the left, *over* the rest of the preceding characters or word, they indicate ardour and rapidity of thought and action, and impulsiveness, though sometimes, notwithstanding, *restraint*.

Should the *d*'s final be curved in a backward direction, it would show mental cultivation, strong powers of imagination, &c., whilst, if it were thus carried, and, in addition, *curled* at its finish in a sort of

FINALS AND COMMENCEMENTS 51

spiral fashion, it would then denote conceit, presumption, pretension, or vanity, as the accompanying signs would warrant one's determining.

If the *d* (capital or small letter) terminates with an undulating throw-off to the right—not in a *loop*, but a *return stroke*—it indicates a coquettish nature, hence love of admiration and a strong desire for approval.

This particular form of final is also said to show constraint. Much, of course, in a case of this kind, would depend upon the accompanying indications.

Angular and ascendant finals show an impatient temperament; but such as are soft-looking and well-rounded indicate a gentle, calm, contemplative nature, as well as, generally speaking, elegance of tastes and perception of form.

Very round, lifeless-looking, and not properly finished-off terminals denote a lethargic, indolent, or even lazy temperament.

Broken and curved final strokes, that is, those which are formed of a succession of *angles,* indicate a total want of artistic taste, also harshness, severity, and want of both culture and tact.

Dwindling or gladiolated final letters, such as become almost indecipherable, or, rather, *disappear* almost, if not quite altogether, show *finesse* and an impenetrable personality, which will be either subtle, hypocritical, or dissimulating, according to the accompanying characteristics.

People who write in this manner to excess are mistrustful, as a rule, though care should be exercised in order to see that the diminishing letters are not due to undue hurry worry, or vivacity.

If the terminals to the letters surround or cover the word of which they form a part, they show, broadly speaking, a protective spirit—a somewhat Quixotic nature, perhaps, but a loyal disposition, for all that.[1] This quality, according to the signs with which it is found, may imply mere self-complacence, pretension, or vanity, however, though it is *seldom, if ever*, to be seen without the trait just described. I generally find that this sign appears more in the letters *b, d, f, t, v, w*, and *y* than in any of the others.

Such finals as are formed by a returning curve that is higher than the letter of which it is part, are said, with what truth I know not, to indicate a lack of judgment.

Highly-raised finals, if *angular*, are said to show a satirical, caustic wit; if *curved*, are stated to indicate a sense of the ridiculous of a more *humorous* and less sarcastic nature.

Personally, from the *trend* of the finals, I always in my own work judge of the *hopefulness*, or the reverse, of the writer.

Thus, with the *up*-turned terminals, one usually

---

[1] Often, I think, this sign denotes a conjugal nature and great constancy in attachment, and, mostly, an intense love of home, children, pets, animals, or flowers, if not all.

FINALS AND COMMENCEMENTS 53

finds a cheerful disposition, and with the *down*-turned ones an unhopeful turn of mind. The faculty of " Hope " will be found to be traceable for its (physical) origin to the liver—so says a well-known writer—though it may be that the state of that organ is referable to the faculty. However that may be, with the up-curved terminals you will generally find an active liver, and with down-turned finals a torpid or diseased one.

If the final strokes are raised in an angular fashion, and in such a way as to fly above the level of the tops of the rest of the characters, an ardent, enthusiastic temperament is always denoted.

When the finals ascend in a straight line, more or less vertically, above the letters, they show a mystical nature, much love of the marvellous and wonderful, and often religious mania.

In-turned finals, such as are formed with a return curve, more especially to the capitals, and *e* and *x*, show selfishness, or, at any rate, egoism, a nature that is incapable of forgetting, much less denying, *self*.

Generally speaking, these inward hooks are seen in the handwritings of insignificant persons, or those of mediocre intellect.

If the finals show at their extremities *very small* hooks, it is said to show tenacity.

If the finals take a sweeping curl, and stretch from left to right, finishing finally with a return downward trend in the reverse direction, they show a resistant, independent nature.

This quality will be manifested either by a pretty petulance, a self-defensive, defiant spirit, or an uncouth brusqueness, according to the rest of the accompanying indications.

Blunt, bludgeon-shaped finals indicate strong will, force of character, extreme determination, and, occasionally, a quarrelsome, contentious nature. Such as "fine" away to a tail-like point, indicate, on the contrary, a want of resolution.

With what degree of correctness, or otherwise, I am hardly prepared to say—as the sign is seldom met with, so far as I have observed, in English handwriting—an American writer states that when the terminals, especially those which belong to such letters as *y* or *g*, are thrown off with a long, extended stroke, that twists itself either above the letter or around the *loop below it*, they denote some personal abnormal error, some bad habit—intemperance, excessive smoking, opium-drugging, and so forth.

If the last letter of a word or syllable should be higher than the rest, it is said to show frankness, candour, and sincerity of purpose. For my own part, I cannot trace the analogy here, though some graphological experts may be able to do so. Certainly, one often *does* see this graphic sign in conjunction with honesty and straightforwardness. Nevertheless, I should not look for the indication of such a qualifica-

FINALS AND COMMENCEMENTS

tion in the rising of the last letter of a word, and I do not advise my readers to do so either.

When the up-strokes of such letters as b, d, f, h, k, l, p, t, &c., are, as a rule, *longer* than the down-strokes of f, g, j, p, q, y, and z, it indicates that the writer's *mental* activity is proportionally greater than his physical. The converse denotes the reverse, viz., that his manual activity exceeds his intellectual.

If the down-strokes of such letters as g, j, &c., &c., are formed in a looped fashion, I generally find that the writer possesses considerable love of home. Whilst when the up-strokes of such letters as b, f, &c., are well looped, they denote, according to my own theories, affection for children, pets, animals, and so on.

When the small h, k, &c., are formed with a long, flowing loop, which attaches them to the rest of the letters, they show sensibility of temperament, likewise loquacity. This graphic sign, I think, is not an *absolute* one, however. Before passing judgment, reference must be made to the rest of the indications afforded by the handwriting under consideration, in order to render a just and true verdict.

VI.

THE LETTERS CONSIDERED GENERALLY, AND THE CHARACTERISTICS DISCLOSED BY THEM

By observing the method of placing the various letters and signs in relation to one another, the intellectual capacity of the subject is to be determined.

Thus, when the letters, &c., are found to be constantly unconnected, and are even disjointed here and there at intervals, the capitals standing alone, the writer will possess excellent mental powers, all else being equal, and the intellectual capacity will be above the average; such faculties as those which give the power of reasoning (both from effect to cause, and from cause to effect), for criticising, comparing, idealising, and for gaining a natural insight into motives and character being highly developed—or, at least, very actively so.

If, on the contrary, they are, as a general principle, united, and the words are run on to one another with a continuous stroke of the pen, it indicates, of course, a proportionate want of the faculties enumerated above; although, notwithstanding, the person who writes in such a fashion may be a very "capable" individual, and possess practical instincts, balanced reasoning powers, conversational gifts, ingenuity, a quick intelligence, an active brain, progressive tendencies, considerable "cleverness," and so on, though he or she can never be as profound as those who write in the former way.

The happy mean is, after all, the best; that is, when there is evidence of both of the graphic signs, some of the letters being united, and others again being not so; for then the writer will be neither "theoretical," "slow," nor "unpractical," nor wanting in acumen or a vein of "idealism;" but, on the contrary, not only capable of gathering, and (what is quite as important) distinguishing between the facts which are seen, but capable of assimilating them and turning his knowledge to good account.

I have asserted in the foregoing paragraph that the unconnected characters imply reasoning capacity, logical ability, ideality of temperament, and spontaneous conception of human nature. It may not, therefore, unreasonably be urged that, in spite of my insisting upon "*one sign, one trait*," I am departing from the precept inculcated elsewhere.

The fact of the matter is, that we shall rarely meet with any specimen of handwriting embracing the above signs which does not at the same time belong to a person possessing all of the characteristics.

But, so that we may at once determine the bias of our subject's mind, we must observe the *type* of handwriting by having recourse to the laws of Form.

Thus, if the sample in any given case be composed principally of the elements of the *line* and *angle*, in addition to having the parted letters, it would show the capacity for comprehending solid, concrete ideas, and thus would denote *philosophy* and *metaphysical* tendencies; whereas, were it to abound in *curves* more especially, then the disjointed characters would indicate more idealistic and imaginative tendencies.

It has been said by previous writers that the *connected* letters denote "deductive" judgment, and such as are *set apart* from one another indicate "intuitive" judgment. It must have been difficult for those who have studied the elements of mind, however, to have reconciled these characteristics with the cranial, facial, or chirological presumably equivalent signs; and, doubtless, many persons have laboured under an entire misapprehension of the faculties really involved.

The terms that are employed by me are apparently the *exact opposite* of those of most other writers; but, in order to explain my position, I will subjoin the following:—

The probable reason why the constantly connected letters have been said to indicate such qualifications as "reasoning-ability," "logical capacity," "sequence and association of ideas," "cohesive thought," &c., is

LETTERS

that a relative lack of the "reflective faculties," which, as I have already shown, are indicated by the separated letters, presupposes a measurable preponderance of the "Perceptive Group," which latter gives, not intellectual powers at all, but *practical* reasoning capabilities, and the gift of seeing the application of principles, and so forth.

In order to acquaint him or herself with the first of these graphic signs, the separated letters, the reader is advised to inspect the autographs of, say, Humboldt, Matthew Arnold, Michael Faraday, Giuseppe Mazzini, William Paley, Talleyrand, Edison, Sir Edwin Arnold, Molière, Joseph Addison, Milton, Shakespeare, Schiller, Fenimore Cooper, Charles Lever, Théophile Gautier, François Coppée, R. D. Blackmore, Sarah Siddons, and Sarah Bernhardt; while for the second, constantly united letters, he or she is referred to those of the following personages: The Prince of Wales, the Right Hon. W. E. Gladstone, H. M. Stanley, Lord Beaconsfield, Edmund Burke, the Emperor of Germany (William II.), David Livingstone, Miss Frances E. Willard, Daniel O'Connell, Sir J. A. Macdonald, E. About, Louis Kossuth, "Stonewall Jackson," Bishop Bossuet, George Canning, Lord Brougham and Vaux, William Pitt, Maria Edgeworth, Wilkie Collins, Charles Dickens, Anthony Trollope, John Stuart Mill, W. Makepeace Thackeray, Sir John Lubbock, Henry Arthur Jones, Thomas Hardy, Sir Rowland Hill, Mrs. Craik, Nat. P. Willis

Sir Walter Besant, Anthony Hope (Hawkins), Björnsterne Björnson, and Sir Henry Irving, to name no others.

Many of the above writers *combine* both signs in their handwritings, although, in every case, that which is pointed out *predominates*.

To recapitulate:—Clear handwriting, the strokes of which present a clear-cut appearance, and are well adjusted, so that they are not confused or entangled one with another, shows lucidity of thought, level-headedness, and clearness of mental vision.

By noting the tracing of the letters, and the direction in and method by which the pen has been employed, the innate quality of the mind can be gauged at once.

Commonplace, coarse, vulgar people use an overplus of ink, exaggerating, complicating, and failing to regulate their mode of forming the letters; whereas superior, unconventional, naturally refined, even if uneducated, persons will, as far as possible, economise the ink in their efforts when writing, by curtailing, sometimes to such a point as to render their "pothooks" and "hangers" indecipherable.

By studying carefully the "pen-tracing" outline in this way, and by taking into consideration whether it is "laboured" and unnecessarily complicated, or the reverse, the grade of mentality can be arrived at at once.

VII.

THE MORE IMPORTANT LETTERS CONSIDERED SINGLY, AND THE LAWS WHICH GOVERN THEM

HAVING considered now the chief points signified by the handwriting *as a whole*, our best plan will be, in the next place, to take the letters one by one, pointing out the special facilities which they afford the graphologist for the analysis of character.

As usual, there are one or two *general* rules to be borne in mind even when proceeding to consider the letters individually.

For instance, when *one* method is adopted exclusively in forming a letter, it points to constancy, non-variableness of mood and behaviour. It is a well-known fact that some people are never twice alike in this particular, whilst others are always the same.

It will be unnecessary to review *every* single letter separately, and, upon the whole, the best plan will be to take a certain number of them, which lend themselves peculiarly to the development of this or that special sign, pointing out the characteristics applicable thereunto, and giving, as further examples, other letters in which the graphological signs are the most likely to occur.

If the capitals be joined to the small letters by which they are followed [some authorities state that this follows the rules given for the connection of the letters generally, viz., sequence of ideas, &c.], the indication is that of an altruistic, kind-hearted individual, possessed of broad sympathies and a large heart. When, however, the capital letter is united with the one (small or otherwise) which follows it, *after describing a loop*, it is said to show that sort of self-sacrifice which believes in the motto "Charity begins at home." Generally speaking, those who write thus, I am led to believe, are clannish. Personally, I believe this trait to be shown by this particular graphic sign, in virtue of its being a loop, which, according to my own theories, always argues a patriotic or home-loving and party-supporting nature. Small, simply-formed capitals imply humility, modesty, though, if excessively low, they would show a cringing, fawning sort of disposition. Disproportionately "swagger" capitals denote an *affected, boastful, conceited nature.*

Elegantly-shaped, curvilinear forms of the letters, capitals especially, are held, by one or two writers, to show artistic taste for *painting.* The *colour-sense*, however, I have generally found allied with considerable *thickness* of the strokes of which the handwriting is formed (which see); consequently I look upon the above sign more as a clue to *general artistic* capacity than anything else, as expounded by the basic laws of Form.

Inharmonious, ungraceful, inelegant characters reveal a want of artistic perception.

The more *severe* in form are the letters—that is, the more they approach those of the printed type—the more will the tastes approximate to architectural tastes. The reason for this is found in the fact that the *typographic* letters do not abound so greatly in *curves* as do those of the cursive "hand," and a good *bony* structure, which is needed for architecture, &c., is not so admirably suited to reproduce *curvilinear* characters as are the tapering fingers of the muscular-built person.

A. a.—The capital: the more it approaches in shape to the printed letter, the greater will be the writer's sense of form, the ability to observe and remember shapes, outlines, and configuration generally. This rule holds good with *all* the letters.

If the typographic form is used decisively, it is said to show a consequential, egoistic nature, but *of itself* it could not do so.

When the two upright strokes are crossed by a thick horizontal line, force of will, executive power, energy, power of endurance, &c., are indicated. (As regards the *form* and *direction* of this line, see the section devoted to the letter *t*.)

If the vertical lines are crossed and united by a *loop*, which turns from right to left around them, a protective nature is denoted, accompanied by, I find, as a rule, love of *children* or affection for pets and animals.

When the letter takes the form of an enlarged small one, and is made by simply a more or less circular movement of the hand *plus* a "pot-hook," it shows an unsophisticated yet clear-minded personality.

The small letter, as well as the last variety, when carefully made and closed up at the top, shows a prudent, reserved nature; when open, loquacity, a want of reserve and indiscretion.

When the *a* is left open at the *bottom*, it indicates dissimulation, or even lying. The same rule applies, with equal force, to the letters *d*, *o*, &c., and will be found to hold good, also, with *n*, *m*, &c., when the *first* and *second*, or *second* and *third*, parts of the letters are *broken* and separate from one another.

B. b.—The capital: if the upper stroke of the second part of the letter over-rides the upright line which it is intended to cross, it indicates love of rule, power, and domination, as well as not a little independence of spirit. Commencing with a short up-stroke, as is not unfrequently the case, the letter would show the desire to amass; if, however, this peculiarity were found in conjunction with a very sloping "hand," it would denote acquisitiveness, more particularly in respect to the *affections;* hence, jealousy.

When this in-turned commencement is seen in combination with a very upright style, it would show extreme egoism, or even right-down *selfishness*, were the letters of an angular description and huddled or crowded together.

The small *b* is of no special importance; but when the up-stroke is *looped*, I generally look for strong motherly or fatherly instincts; whilst, if the final be twisted to the right, in such a manner as to make a kind of "pocket," prior to its uniting itself with the following character, the foregoing sign is intensified.

If, as is sometimes the case, the second up-stroke or final is turned to the left, so as nearly to *close* the body of the letter, it indicates extreme secrecy in design.

C. c.—This letter, small and capital alike, in the same way as *a, d, e, g, o, q,* and *x*, and (sometimes) *s, v, w,* and *y*, will indicate (inasmuch as in its *true* form it partakes of the element of the curve) such qualities as artistic feeling, sentiment of temperament, emotion, intuition, affection, imagination, and enthusiasm. Being (normally) of an *oval* shape, this letter is especially well adapted to portray the aforementioned traits, and will do so in proportion as it is formed after a curvilinear plan. The more rectilinear the type of letter, the less will it indicate such characteristics as the foregoing.

E. e.—The capital, except that it lends itself peculiarly to flourish, is not more significant than the rest of the letters, the rules applicable to which hold good in respect to it. When, however, a loop is formed prior to its connection with the following letters, it shows no lack of affection, but *clannishness*. These writers, though they may be kind and well-disposed, would invariably inculcate the motto, " Look after your own first, and outsiders afterwards."

If made after the printed type of letter, the *E* would indicate, in virtue of its being composed exclusively of a series of *straight lines*, such traits of character as reason, intellect, rectitude, stability, order, and conservatism; also scientific or mechanical, as opposed to artistic tastes.

The small *e*, if so formed that its "eye" or loop is clearly-cut and not "blind," would show lucidity of thought; if so shaped as to be what is termed an "open" letter, it would indicate candour and frankness.

The *Greek e*, as well as the *d*, when formed like a Greek *d* (delta), &c., shows mental cultivation.

G. g.—The big *G* will follow the rules prescribed for the letter *C*. The more looped the commencement, the more tender and affectionate the disposition.

Sometimes the down-stroke finishes with a return curve which runs up alongside the *right* hand thereof without crossing it. This is said to imply generosity, and often eccentricity of manner as well. This rule applies with equal force to such letters as *q* and *y*.

If the small letter *g*'s loop be excessively long, it

would indicate exaggeration; if disproportionately full and wide, imagination.

The above rules will be found to apply particularly to the letters *j, q, y,* and *z.*

H. h.—The capital, if formed after the looped pattern, will indicate such characteristics as I have shown are peculiar to all such shaped characters, viz., sensitiveness, love of animals, children, friends, or home, &c.

The *H*, however, when made after the fashion of the *printed* letter, will indicate, according to the parallelism of the two upright strokes, the degree of the writer's judgment of size, measurement, bulk, proportion, and distance.

[1] When the two upright lines are spread out far apart, they show force of character, boldness, self-dependence; when they are compressed, they denote weakness, inertitude.

Of the small *h* little need be said, as it will follow the rules applicable to such letters as *b, f, k,* &c.

I. i.—The capital letter is comparatively unimportant, and may be left with safety to the judgment of the student, who will be able to apply the laws which govern it with perfect ease.

No letter, out of the whole twenty-six in the English alphabet, is more significant than the small *i*.

---

[1] This rule holds good also with regard to the *width* of any of the letters, &c. Narrow, lanky-looking characters showing feebleness, want of staying power, and so on.

68 THE LANGUAGE OF HANDWRITING

The body of the letter, of course, follows exactly the same rules as regards its formation as do those of the rest of the characters, but the "dotting" of the *i* is of *special* importance.

The *proper* position for the dot to occupy is that directly *above* the first of the strokes of which the letter is composed. When placed precisely in this spot, it signifies attention to *minutiæ*, reflection, and good judgment.

Put on the *right* side of the letter, in advance of it, in fact, the dot indicates a precipitate, ardent, happy-go-lucky nature, also a want of forethought; when placed *behind*, on the *left* side of the letter, it shows, on the contrary, an apprehensive, over-careful, and nervous disposition.

When the dot is set at a great height above the letter, it indicates ambition, high aspirations, and a strong imagination; if, on the other hand, it be placed low down, the reverse will be the case, and the writer will be precise, "particular," seldom carried away by enthusiasm or hero-worship, and rarely of a "romantic" or visionary state of mind. Generally speaking, when the dot is placed in the latter manner, the writer will have considerable powers of mental concentration, and the capacity for protracted attention and study in some one direction.

Left undotted altogether, the *i* indicates an untidy, heedless, slovenly person.

As regards the *shape* of the dot, if well rounded

and evenly made, it would show prudence : if it were, instead of that, angular and irregular in form, it would denote irritability and a more or less excitable temperament.

If very *thick*, the dot to the *i* would indicate materialism, or, at any rate, a nature such as this world's enjoyments would appeal to strongly. Very often, if *extremely* large and heavy, this sort of dot indicates an ungovernable temper, warmth of nature and strong passions always, if not an absolutely brutal tendency.

If, as is frequently the case, the dots vary in emphasis, they are said to show *animation*.

Of course it is quite unnecessary to mention that these remarks apply with equal force to the letter *j*, besides to any of the rest of the stops, colons, semicolons, commas, &c., &c., met with.

L. l.—The capital: if so made that the *base*,[1] *i.e.*, the loop, &c., formed at the side of and below the down-stroke, is enlarged, it indicates a self-satisfied, boastful nature ; or, if formed in such a way that the main-stroke of the letter is *raised up* above the lower part thereof, it is said to denote " pride of comparison."

The small *l*'s rules differ in no way from those laid down for such letters as *b, f, h,* &c.

[1] The fact of the base of this letter, as of *Q, X,* &c., taking a *looped* form at all would indicate, apart from any other characteristics disclosed by its actual shape, such qualities as are applicable to the looped *f*'s, *g*'s, *j*'s, &c. &c., viz., "inhabitiveness," &c.

N. n.—The capital: when the first stroke,[1] " ascension," or " head " is " drawn up " above that which follows it, it indicates " proper pride ; "[2] if it be *lower* than the rest, it indicates either satisfied ambition or pretension, envious pride, or force of character or modesty.

When the points are of *equal* height, it shows a calm nature, self-complacence, and contentment, as well as orderliness, consideration, and so forth.

If the base of the letter should be *wide*, and the strokes be placed far apart, it indicates vigour, independence, self-satisfaction, arrogance, or self-esteem ; when *narrow*, it would show constraint, timidity, disquietude, and feebleness of character.

The letters *H, M, U, V, W,* and *Y* more especially follow the above rules, also *D*, &c.

When the small *n* is formed after the shape of a *u*, it indicates suavity, kindliness, and so forth, a " hail-fellow-well-met " nature.

It will be noticed, after careful consideration, that the movement which serves to produce this shape of the letter is an *under-handed* one (literally) from left to right.

When the reverse is the case, therefore, and the letters are produced by an *over-handed* motion, I generally look for a bluff but honest nature.

---

[1] No matter whether the letter be formed after either the old or the new pattern.

[2] If, however, this should be due to the following " shoulder " of the letter almost *disappearing*, it would more especially indicate *finesse*.

IMPORTANT LETTERS

The Archbishop of Canterbury writes a style in which the latter type of letter is conspicuous.

Exactly the same rule will be found to apply to such letters as *h, m, p, r, w, y*, &c.

S. s.—The *S* is unremarkable; but the more looped it is, the more capacity for tenderness in the nature of the writer.

If the final turn inward, the greater will be the egoism of the person—the more inclined will he or she be to feel slights, and the less self-sacrificing the disposition.

If the small *s* is fashioned after the old style, and composed of two loops run together—the upper, of a stroke from left to right, and the lower, of a stroke from right to left—it would show extreme gentleness of nature, and probably an utter incapacity on the part of the writer to stick up for himself or assert his just claims.

Such a character, unless other contradictory signs were well in evidence, would be very liable to be imposed and played upon.

T. t.—The *capital*, if made so that the top-stroke flies above it, shows indolence of temperament, as well as vivid powers of fancy, and, as a rule, a somewhat dogmatic, tyrannical, dictatorial nature. When formed *all in one piece*, the top attaching itself to the other portion of the letter, it shows a simple, natural disposition, also directness of insight.

In all other respects—such as the way in which

the crossbar commences, and terminates—the rules applicable to the *small* letter (as under) are equally so to the capital.

In the *small* letter, the down-stroke follows the rules given for those of the rest of the letters; consequently, it will be noticed incidentally only. The real significance of the *t* resides in the *barring* or *crossing*, which tells of the writer's will-power, energy, and " temper "—among other important points to which we shall have occasion to refer.

With reference to the *length* of the crossing, the following are the chief indications :—

The Bar.

Long, fine, and of equal thickness throughout = Energy, ardour, ambition.

Long and crossing two or three letters = Impulse.

Long, thicker at *finish* than *start*, and *crushed down* upon other small letters = Arbitrary will.

Sometimes long and at *other times short*—almost, now and again, a mere dot = Imagination, fantasy.

Flying into the letters of the next word = Animation, impulse, vivacity, sequence of ideas, jovial nature.

Strong and thicker than down-stroke = Great determination and self-will.

Short and thick and crushed down, as it were = Contrariness of thought and action, strength of mind.

IMPORTANT LETTERS

Long t-bars show, generally, animation and spirit; while such as are *short*, reveal energy — though, personally, I generally look for the degree of "executiveness"—resistance, resolution, and combativeness—in the *presence* of the crossing; whilst upon its *thickness* I have located the faculty of "destructiveness," energy, force, thoroughness, power of endurance, capacity for severity and hatred. Consequently, when the cross-bar fails to extend in front of the upright stroke, and is visible only at the *left*-hand side thereof, it shows a slow, hesitating, procrastinating nature; whereas, when it reaches to the right-hand side of the line, it indicates that the initiative faculty is present in a corresponding degree.

(Oliver Cromwell barred even his "*l*'s," as did Blücher, and the late Duke of Argyll also.)

If the bar is *absent altogether*,[1] it indicates an acquiescent nature, devoid of all force of character, and with little, if any, of the resistive element in the composition.

Persons whose *t*'s are *uniformly* without any crossing, dislike struggle, and need to be "backed up," and taken by the hand, in order that they may not succumb under difficulties.

When the *t* is not only *minus* a bar, but without

---

[1] In such a case, however, it would be necessary to inspect the rest of the graphological signs, such as dashes, bars, hyphens, lines across such letters as the capitals *A*, *H*, *F*, *T*, and some small letters, &c., &c. (if present), to which the rules apply with equal force.

a *loop* as well, and the letter is of a *rounded* type too, it indicates a total want of energy, an utter lack of will-power, and generally a careless indifference of nature.

When, as is perhaps more generally the case, the bar is absent *in conjunction with an angular final-stroke* to the letter, it indicates, not necessarily either negligence or want of spirit, but rather a lack of *initiatory* will-power, and, of course, some obstinacy —which will always be present in a character of the type—in its place.

When the *t* is sometimes barred, and at others left uncrossed, it indicates irresolution, a rather vacillating, undecided disposition, a " postponer."

The real thing of importance, of course, to consider in connection with the *t*-bar, when in evidence, is its *thickness*, strength, or slenderness.

The Bar. — *Thick* = vigour : *in excess, violence ;* great capacity for indignation. If, in addition, it be *long*—ill-considered effort or inability ; if *short*— great force. *Thin* = want of vigour ; *in excess*, want of force of character.[1] If, in addition, it be *long*— feeble will-power ; if *short*—small will and want of decision.

As often as not, however, the crossings not only vary in thickness here and there in a single case, but absolutely maintain no consistent regularity of outline at all. In such instances the following rules will hold good :—

---

[1] For more explicit rules see farther on.

IMPORTANT LETTERS

When the bar is irregular in shape, it indicates a rather capricious, volatile, unstable character, such as is hardly to be depended upon. On the contrary, therefore, when it is uniformly *thick* and *regular* in its outline, it indicates quiet decision, calmness, composure, temperance, and such-like attributes.

When the bar is of exactly *equal* length on either side of the upright stroke which it crosses—that is, it advances as far to the right hand as it retreats on the left—it is said to indicate a persevering turn of mind; whilst, should it be *longer* in front on the right-hand side of the line, it is stated to show patience.

These graphic signs, however, I consider to be auxiliary and not *absolute* ones.

The shape of the cross-bar will be found to vary considerably, even in a single case.

The Bar.

Curved and placed over vertical stroke	= Affectation.
Partaking of the nature of a flourish	= Imagination, egoism.
In the form of the lash of a whip	= Effusiveness, fancy.
Curved	= Irresolution, kindness, delicacy, restraint over the feelings.
Formed like a serpentine line	= Gaiety, merriment, mercy, grace.

76 THE LANGUAGE OF HANDWRITING

The *position* of the bar, as well as its extent, is also very important.

PLACED.

High up	= Ambition.
High up and firm	= Dyspepsia.
Nearly at the top of the vertical line, but not flying above it	= Determined despotism of opinion.
Above the upright stroke [1]	= Imperiousness, *or* arbitrariness.
Over letter and curved, so that it overrides the letter flying *above* it.	= Hastiness, capriciousness, impatience, self-will.
High and "tailing" off	= Vivacity, quick nature.
Low down	= Slow nature, obstinacy.
Low, and crossing tops of other letters	= Hasty temper, strong will.
Very low down	= Obedience, humbleness, resignation.

The manner in which the bar terminates follows the rules applicable to the rest of the finals.

THE BAR.

Trending up	= Optimism.
Trending down	= Pessimism.
Up-tending and small and jerky	= Imitation, mimicry.
"Crooked," or ending in a hook-like finish	= Tenacity of purpose.

---

[1] When the head of the *P* is formed of a flourishing, open circle, which is put over the straight down-stroke, it also indicates pride and a tendency to despotism.

IMPORTANT LETTERS

Finishing in a rounded curve	= Gentleness, want of will-power, absence of persistence, grace of mind, a yielding and refined nature, artistic perception of beauty.
Ending in a point	= Criticism, malice, causticity, liability to go to extremes in feeling, &c.
Fining away at the termination	= A want of perseverance.
Turning *up* very much at its finish	= Ill-will, malice.
Ending in a thick finish	= Energy, vivaciousness, strong will, obstinacy, perseverance, an ardent temperament
Terminating in a club-like stroke	= Resolution *or* violence.

Although the up-slanting *t*-bar, which ascends in a more or less straight (oblique) line, has been said, by different writers, to show such characteristics as captiousness of temperament, quarrelsomeness, a disposition to argue and have "the last word," and a contradictious nature; or, on the other hand, ardour of spirit, dash, heedlessness, and a "happy-go-lucky" turn, according to circumstances, I consider that, when *excessively* developed in a handwriting, such a style of crossing indicates a species of *obliquity*, and, therefore, does *not* show such admirable qualities as those that are placed in the latter list. Thomas Carlyle, a genius certainly, but one "struck by lightning," as Ruskin has truly said, wrote very up-slanting *t*-bars, which were highly suggestive of his cavilling, spiteful temper, and his distorted mental vision, which made those around him appear to him mostly as "fools," as he tactfully put it, when he expressed himself upon the subject.

Figures.

The *Roman* numerals, of course, follow the rules applicable to the letters, while the *Arabic* are not specially important. Yet, as to despise the "minute" is to despise the "infinite," they claim a passing glance.

The figures, from their very nature, it will be found, lend themselves with peculiar facility to the laws of the principles of *Form;* the *curve* (sphere and ovoid) being particularly exemplified in 2, 3, 5, 6, 8, 9, and 0; and the *line* (angle and square) in 1, 4, and 7.

The figures 1, 2, 3, 6, 7, 8, 9, and 0 call for no comment; but it may be observed of 4, that, when the second (horizontal) line is crossed by a separate down-stroke, it shows care, attention, and prudence; also, of 5, that when the top-stroke (the "nightcap"), is present, and placed duly on the right side of the letter, it indicates habits of neatness. This will also indicate, according to its thickness, &c., the state of the writer's temper.

IMPORTANT LETTERS

By being *united*, the figures will express cohesion of ideas, consecution of thought, and so on.

Their *separation* will, of course, denote the exact opposite, provided that "all else is equal."

Signs, &c.

When the ambersand (&) is *looped* in a high degree, there will be a protective, loyal nature present: otherwise, the reverse.

The apostrophes, accents, and quotation marks (" inverted commas ") follow the rules given for the dot to the *i*; that is, according to their *height* will they show the writer's power of veneration (even to verging on superstition); and by their *roundness* or *angularity* respectively, his or her placidity or excitability.

When such marks are thick, they indicate strong passions, ardour, and so forth; if they be delicately formed, they would show the reverse.

When dots are interspersed, *where not required*, throughout a MS., it indicates difficulty in breathing.

When the full stops or periods (.), as well as all commas (,), colons (:), semicolons (;), parentheses ( ), brackets [ ], hyphens (-), &c., are in their proper places, they show methodical habits, due regard for order, and a systematic nature.

Inattention to the foregoing would indicate a heedless character and lack of detail; also, generally speaking, a bad memory.

If bars are substituted for stops, it shows prudence and guardedness.

When they are placed at the ends of sentences, *in addition* to full stops, they then indicate a mistrustful, and very watchful nature.

When notes of " admiration " or " exclamation " (!), and interrogation (?), and dashes, &c., are interspersed throughout the handwriting specimen, it denotes a tendency to magnify and embellish, to " enthuse," and wax warm upon such topics as the writer has " at heart." The misuse of such signs would imply a thorough want of " balance," and a tendency to let the imagination " run riot,"—this, because of their employment being *abnormal*.

"Touched up" letters (such as *r* made in the shape of *i* being surmounted by a little stroke made with a separate pen-movement, or *H*, for example, made after the form of the printed letter and then retouched and finished off by having two little bars placed, one above and one below it) indicate a love of perfection; and are also said to show " a habit of reverting to the first idea;" such characters do not believe there is " no room for improvement."

Ill-finished letters, on the contrary, indicate but limited notions in regard to matters of finish, and usually pertain to those who think anything " will do," and that their work is as good as " it need be."

Such persons, if novelists, think that *quantity* (*i.e.,* so many thousand words per diem, and such-and-such a number of works per annum), exceeds in importance the *quality* (*i.e.*, originality of treatment and style) of their productions. Wilkie Collins, Charles Dickens, Thackeray, Sir Edwin Arnold, Thomas Hardy, Dr. Conan Doyle, and Mr. W. S. Gilbert, all noted for sound and thorough workmanship, wrote and write exceedingly carefully-constructed " hands."

VIII.

FLOURISHES

MUCH might be written upon the subject of flourishes, for so diversified are their forms, and so varied are the modes of appending them to the letters, that each fresh one seen forms a study of itself.

The following observations, however, will be found to hold good in respect to most flourishes ; as, when any are observed to present *several* of the peculiarities mentioned in combination, a little trouble on the student's part will serve to translate their signification.

First of all, it must be said that *all* flourishes denote some degree of egoistical feeling, though I have not found (as some writers profess to have done) that they show *self-satisfaction* or conceit, but, on the contrary, that they indicate rather a desire *for being praised, love of approbation,* and so forth.

Shapeless, vulgar flourishes, sorry attempts at ornamentation, unbecoming embellishments and paraphs, such as are out of all keeping with their environments, show little else than a common mind, a " would be " *if* " you could " person—a " snob."

A " cob-webbed " flourish is said to show skill in

COBWEBBED.
(Eugène Beauharnais.)

ZIG-ZAG.
(Zola, Jerome
Bonaparte,
Charles Kingsley.)

LASSO-LIKE.
(Bonaparte, Moreau, Nelson,
Pellisier, Outram, Soult,
Charlotte Corday, H. M. Stanley.)

ATTACKING.
(Cornwallis, Lord Roberts,
Sir John Moore.)

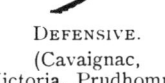

DEFENSIVE.
(Cavaignac,
Victoria, Prudhomme,
Zola, Doré.)

COURAGEOUS.
(Gambetta,
Spurgeon.)

ELABORATE.

COMPLICATED.
(Don Carlos, Lord Bacon.)

SERPENTINE.

FENCING.

Face p. 82a]

WITTY.

(Sterne, "Mark Twain," Eliza Cook, Cruikshank, Hood, F. C. Burnand Dickens, Beaconsfield, Sir Wilfrid Lawson, "Phiz," Hogarth, Edw. Lear.)

(William II. of Germany.)

CORKSCREW.
(Pope Leo XIII.)

(Sir Robert Walpole.)

CAREFUL.

COQUETTISH
(Patti, Albani, Bernhardt, Mrs. Kendal, Mrs. Langtry, Kyrle Bellew, Coppée, Ristori, Duchess of York.)

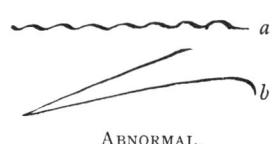

ABNORMAL.

(*a*. Garibaldi; *b*. Sir Arthur Sullivan.)

[*Face p.* 82*b*

FLOURISHES

affairs, and if such a one is crossed by a stroke which terminates in a kind of hook, it shows a grasping, selfish nature.

When the flourish is zigzagged, and approaches in shape the pattern of " forked lightning " (not the *real* thing, by the way, but what artists have generally given us to understand was forked lightning), it shows activity of a very pronounced description.

A lasso-like flourish indicates self-assertion, but the precise signification of the lines of which it is composed will depend upon their *direction* and *contour*.

When at the end of the name a stroke runs down, by way of flourish, it shows egoism.

If the signature terminates with a line from *left* to *right*, it indicates a defiant, aggressive spirit; if it ends with one that slants in the opposite direction, from *right* to *left*, it shows a defensive nature; whilst when it finishes with a stroke that *descends* vertically, it then denotes a brave, courageous disposition, such as "never says die " or " gives in."

An elaborate flourish shows vanity, love of display, ostentation, affectation, and boastfulness.

Complicated flourishes show mistrust and subtlety of nature, and such as are formed of intertwined lines bespeak an intriguing personality.

A symmetrical, serpentine flourish (one end of which turns upward and the other down) shows *verve*, imagination, and love of effect.

When the flourish takes the form of a line which

fences in the signature above and below, it shows a "reasoning selfishness"— personal instincts of an exclusive kind.

A wavy, curved flourish shows a witty, mirthful turn of mind, high spirits, and good-humour.

What has been termed a "snail-shell" flourish, from the fact of its enclosing the whole signature, shows an egoistical, pretentious nature, and great abilities for looking after the interests of "No. 1"— self.

A corkscrew-like flourish, such as begins with a wide spiral movement and tapers off gradually, shows *finesse*, power to manage—"to work the oracle."

A line which closes round the signature, like the jaws of a wild beast, is said to show self-interestedness, and the reason for its thus indicating the estimable qualification is not far to seek. Excessive *Secretiveness*, which, of course, these *surrounding* pen-sweeps denote, argues *impenetrability*, which shows a close or even penurious nature, hence the reverse of kind-heartedness or liberality.

A curved line, commencing and terminating in a sort of looped *hook*, set underneath the signature, shows love of admiration, coquetry, often a love of flirtation, and generally self-complacence.

Two horizontal lines, between which are two little marks or dots, show love of finish and a careful regard for detail.

FLOURISHES

A single simple line placed below the signature [1] may show variously caution, pride of name, or even vanity, according to the accompanying characteristics suggested. I generally find it shows prudence, sense of reputation, and that sense of character that will not let itself down in any way, or suffer its honour to be questioned.

When the words are frequently underlined, it indicates self-esteem, a tendency to exaggerate, enthusiasm, a want of deliberation, and poor judgment.

If the flourish habitually takes any outlandish or abnormal shape, it then indicates marked individuality.

A complete absence of flourish of any kind whatsoever indicates a want of self-consciousness, "aristocratic" or proper pride, dignity, and an absence of all showfulness.

It had been intended to give a chart illustrative of the principal features of the handwriting—which may be said to consist in: (1) the thickness of the strokes, (2) their slope, (3 and 4) the shapes and sizes of the letters, and (5) the position of the lines in relation to the paper—as have already been treated.

Finding, however, that any such arrangement would only complicate matters, and confuse, rather than

---

[1] According to the manner in which this terminates, &c., will it indicate such characteristics as the writer's will power, and so on. See section on the letter *t*.

enlighten, the student, it has been deemed preferable to cite the following autographs as illustrative of the various points:—

HANDWRITING.

THICKNESS
- Thick—Wilson Barrett (p. 167).
- Neutral—Rev. Newman Hall (p. 193).
- Fine—Mrs. Besant (p. 176).

SLOPE
- Slanting—Hilda Wilson (p. 237).
- Vertical—Andrew Lang (p. 210).
- Backhand—"Cheiro" (p. 180).

LETTERS.

SHAPE
- Rectilinear—Sir S. Wilks (p. 234).
- Ovoid—Lord Leighton (p. 155).
- Circular—Sir Lewis Morris (p. 218).

SIZE
- Large—Rev. Joseph Parker (p. 152).
- Medium—Max O'Rell (p. 225).
- Small—Sir L. Alma-Tadema (p. 162).

LINES.

POSITION
- Ascendant—Sir S. Bancroft (p. 165).
- Horizontal (normal)—Sir G. Newnes (p. 153).
- Descendant—Sir H. Irving (*Frontispiece*).

The real difficulty, it should be added, in practice, lies not so much in testing the *absolute* value of the indications, as in gauging their *relative* strength.

Explanatory of the signs of the 42 Faculties.

~~Amativeness.~~
Conjugality.
~~Friendship.~~
Inhabitiveness.
Philoprogenitiveness.

Acquisitiveness.
~~Alimentiveness.~~
~~Combativeness~~
~~Destructiveness~~
Secretiveness.
~~Vitativeness~~

~~Approbativeness~~

Cautiousness =
Concentrativeness.
Self Esteem.

Benevolence
Conscientiousness
Firmness —
~~Hope~~
Spirituality.
Veneration.

Constructiveness.
Ideality.
Imitation.
Mirthfulness.

Sublimity.
Agreeableness.
Causality.
Comparison.
Eventuality =
Human Nature —
Calculation.
Colour.
FORM.
Individuality.
Language.
Locality

Order.
Size.
Time.
Tune
Weight.

[Face p. 87

IX.

THE FORTY-TWO MENTAL FACULTIES, WITH THEIR GRAPHICAL SIGNS

NOTE.

THE brain, which is the organ of the mind, is essentially a unit, but composed of a collection of *organs*.

There are, at least, forty-two distinct mental faculties; and these now will be described, together with their separate indications in the handwriting.

The reasons for several of the graphological signs are known, and, where it has been possible to do so, these will be found given.

There exists in the brain a "writing-centre," through which the operation of transcribing manuscript is carried out. Were this organ to become injured in any way, its function would become impaired.

I.—THE SOCIAL AND DOMESTIC GROUP.

1. AMATIVENESS = *Love of the opposite sex; physical love; sexual love.*

This passion is indicated according to the *thickness* of the writing *as a whole*.

When the strokes are very dark, the character will be sensual and governed by the mere animal propensities; whilst when they are light or of moderate thickness, the nature will be, in proportion, less dominated by the amatory instincts.

Persons who are well-sexed have vigorous, healthy organisations. They possess abundant warmth and force of feeling, which, consequently, makes itself manifest in the handwriting by proportionate thickness of the strokes of the letters of which it is composed. As the function proves the basis of physical being, it is not strange that its development should be gauged according to the thickness (or practically the greater or less *existence*) of the lines.

EXAMPLE.[1]

H. G. R. MIRABEAU (French orator, statesman, and author), 1749–1791. Conspicuous graphical sign, AMATIVENESS: indicated by the black aspect of the writing.

Here Language, Form, Size, Colour, and Artistic reason are well defined.

Sublimity and Ideality, as well as Constructiveness, Hope, Spirituality, Alimentiveness, Vitativeness, Secretiveness, Acquisitiveness, Destructiveness, and Appropativeness, combine to give a thoroughly emotional, sensational, magnetic, and passionate personality, with which the subject has always been credited.

[1] The examples will be found on frontispiece.

THE MENTAL FACULTIES

2. CONJUGALITY = *Constancy in the affections; exclusiveness of attachment.*

Conjugality is indicated (principally) according to the slope of the letters, and in proportion as they incline to the right, as well as by the *consistency* of the handwriting; and the more the individual letters are formed after a set pattern, the more evenly the *t*'s are crossed and the more refined and stable the writing, as a whole, the stronger will be the manifestation of the trait. One particular sign is the bar of the *t* terminating in the form of a barbed hook. *Wide* letters, provided they are formed in a consistent manner, denote more of the quality than narrow ones.

The more responsive the disposition, the greater will be the slope of the handwriting to the right—the pen-movement productive of a very inclined style being *outward* rather than either inward or backward. The consistency of the method in constructing the letters explains itself, and shows singleness of mind and an absence of changeability.

EXAMPLE.

H. M. QUEEN VICTORIA (Queen of the United Kingdom and Empress of India), born in 1819, in England.

Noticeable graphical sign, CONJUGALITY: revealed by the consistent style, well-barred *t*, &c. Language,

Form, Size, Weight, Colour, Order, Time, Tune, Locality, Eventuality, Comparison, Human Nature, Ideality, and Sublimity are all very conspicuous; as are also Benevolence, Conscientiousness, Firmness, Marvellousness, and Veneration. Self-esteem is exceedingly well defined, and added to her great executive capacities, sustentative powers, social disposition, and innate wisdom, causes her to manifest the administrative ability for which she has had no equal.

3. FRIENDSHIP = *Love of society; desire for friendship; the inclination to be in the company of others.*

Friendship is denoted by the *spacing out* of the letters; and the *further they are set apart* the greater will be the manifestation of the trait. When, on the contrary, the letters are huddled together, or are placed very close to one another, the quality will be relatively weak.

Persons who have expansive, genial natures show they possess such by extending their sympathies and good feeling to others; consequently their *movements* are free and easy, unconstrained and without effort; their *arm* works rapidly forward, with the result that an open, spaced-out handwriting is produced.

THE MENTAL FACULTIES

EXAMPLE.

LORD AVEBURY (Sir JOHN LUBBOCK) (banker, savant, and author), born in England, 1834. Conspicuous graphical sign, FRIENDSHIP: shown by the width between the letters. The law of the curve and straight line is the governing principle in this autograph, wherein are observed the signs of Amativeness, Parental Love, Inhabitiveness, Wit, Imitation, Constructiveness, Ideality, Language, Eventuality, Reason, Conscientiousness, Hope, Benevolence, Self-Esteem, and Agreeableness. Altogether, an interesting and talented specimen.

4. INHABITIVENESS = *The love of home and country; the desire to locate oneself in a given place.*

This trait is indicated, I believe, more especially by the letters taking, where it is practicable for them to do so, a looped form. When, for example, the vertical strokes of such letters as *f*, *g*, *j*, *y*, and *z*, &c., are curved and looped before being attached to the letters which follow them, this characteristic will be relatively well defined.

This sentiment is allied to continuity; and, therefore, as the feeling is of a sensitive and sentimental description, the continual joining of the letters to each other *by means of loops*, is manifestly its natural expression in the handwriting.

EXAMPLE.

JAMES FENIMORE COOPER (American novelist), 1789–1851. Noteworthy graphical sign, INHABITIVENESS: shown by the soft, looped style (remark the *p*). The law of the straight line, square, and curve rules this autograph. The signs of Amativeness, Parental Love, Friendship, Benevolence, Veneration, Conscientiousness, Firmness, Ideality, Wit, Imitation, Causality, Comparison, Eventuality, Human Nature, Form, Size, Colour, and Order are highly developed.

5. PHILOPROGENITIVENESS OR PARENTAL LOVE = *Love for children; love of animals.*

The love of children and pets is shown by the looping to the left the strokes of such letters as lend themselves to the treatment. When, for example, the upstrokes of *b, h, d, l, &,* &c., are formed in this manner, and, above all, when the letters *t, A, D, H, f,* and *P,* &c., are *crossed* by means of a loop which turns to the left, and then returns to the right, this trait will be relatively conspicuous. The characteristic is also displayed when the terminals, for instance, close with a return stroke, surrounding the word or letter to which they belong.

Gentle, tender-hearted people are constructed after a *curved* rather than an angular plan; the sweep of

THE MENTAL FACULTIES 93

the pen *to the left* is the graphic sign for *defensiveness*, and, when the stroke describes the segment of a circle, and sweeps in that direction, protectiveness and the love of the young or animals is surely indicated thereby.

EXAMPLE.

The PRINCESS OF WALES. Born in Denmark, 1844. Principal graphical sign, PARENTAL LOVE: exhibited in the looped formation of the letters *a, l, d*, and *f* particularly. The law of the straight line and curve rules this autograph. Inhabitiveness, Amativeness, Approbativeness, Conscientiousness, Hope, Benevolence, Veneration, Form, Size, Colour, Order, Tune, Ideality, Imitation, and Constructiveness are marked.

II.—THE SELFISH PROPENSITIES.

6. ACQUISITIVENESS = *The love of possessions; the sense of property; the desire to accumulate.*

Acquisitiveness has three divisions —

(1) *Power to acquire* is shown by the presence of a hook or "tick" (*i.e.*, an up-stroke at the commencement of the letters).

(2) *Saving, economy,* is indicated in proportion as the words are set nearer to each other.

(3) *Hoarding* is denoted according to the curtailment of the finals.

94 THE LANGUAGE OF HANDWRITING

Those who possess a keen love for providing for the future will be found to display a judicious expenditure even of ink and paper quite spontaneously; whereas improvident, extravagant persons will waste their writing materials, using ridiculously long terminals, and leaving tremendous spaces between the words and lines, or between the top edge of the paper and where they begin to write.

EXAMPLE.

ALEXANDRE DUMAS (*fils*) (French novelist and dramatic writer), 1824–1896. Principal graphical sign, ACQUISITIVENESS: exhibited in the short upstroke with which the *D* commences, and the " docked " finals. Language, Form, Size, Colour, Order, Reasoning - power, Constructiveness and Ideality, which are prominently displayed, proclaim high literary abilities; Approbativeness, Caution, Secretiveness, Destructiveness, Conscientiousness, Firmness, Friendship, and Amativeness are decided.

7. ALIMENTIVENESS = *The sense of hunger and thirst; the love of eating and imbibing.*

As a rule, the appetite of a person may be determined by inspecting the *thickness* of the handwriting generally; when the strokes are proportionately dark, there will be a relatively heartier, healthier appetite

THE MENTAL FACULTIES

than when they are fine and light. Gluttony is signified by intensely muddy, swollen strokes.

A full development of the vital system engenders a proportionately hearty appetite; therefore, as the pen-movement with those of this type is strong, so the writing is, in like manner, thick to the extent of the qualification.

EXAMPLE.

ALEXANDRE DUMAS (*père*) (French novelist and dramatist), born 1803; died 1830. Prominent graphical sign, ALIMENTIVENESS: shown by the black, heavy pen-tracing. The law of the square, curve, and sphere presides over this autograph. Ideality, Constructiveness, Imitation, Language, Form, Size, Order, Reason, Locality, Human Nature, Approbativeness, Benevolence, Conscientiousness, and Friendship all find strong representation here.

8. COMBATIVENESS = *Argumentativeness; assertiveness; courage; defence; pugnacity.*

Combativeness has three divisions—

(1) *Courage* is indicated by a *forward* movement of any of the strokes, the bars to the *t*'s, and a pen-thrust or sweep to the right of any of the finals, &c.

(2) *Defence* is denoted by the bars to the *t*'s slanting *downward*, and also by the terminals trending *backward*, or sweeping under or over the words to the *left*.

(3) *Defiance* is indicated by the bars to the *t*'s taking an upward slant, as well as by a rather upward movement and well-articulated method of writing generally.

N.B.—When the letter *t* is left altogether uncrossed, the indication is that of a timid, non-aggressive nature, especially if the terminals do not exhibit the traces of any remarkable pressure of the pen having been employed.

Quite involuntarily the hand of the combative, resistant individual sweeps either right or left, as he or she is *contrary* or merely *protective*. The *spirit* and natural fearlessness of the writer occasions him to use his pen freely and without extra deliberation; it is driven with emphasis, varying in degree with the extent of the characteristic denoted.

Example.

MARTIN LUTHER (priest, author, and German leader of the Protestant Reformation). Born in Saxony, 1483; died in 1546. Conspicuous graphical sign, COMBATIVENESS: shown by the aggressive characters, the widespread *M*, the forward sweep of the base of the *L*, &c, The law of the straight line and square governs this truly remarkable autograph, which denotes great force of character, heroic zeal, fortitude, and immense determination. The indications of **Amativeness, Parental Love, Inhabitiveness, Friend-**

THE MENTAL FACULTIES

ship, Conscientiousness, Firmness, Veneration, Hope, Benevolence, Destructiveness, Self-esteem, Approbativeness, Language, Order, Eventuality, Causality, Comparison, Human Nature, Wit, Constructiveness, and Sublimity are all pre-eminent, and reveal at once the strength of Luther's personality, his moral, mental, and physical courage, and forcible individuality.

9. DESTRUCTIVENESS = *Executiveness ; force ; thoroughness ; energy ; latent power ; intensity and warmth of feeling ; the inclination to crush and destroy.*

The more forcible the handwriting and club-like the strokes, and the more it is endowed with a forward movement, the larger will be this faculty. This trait is also chiefly to be gauged from the manner in which the letter *t* is barred. When the crossing is absent or only feebly indicated, there will be a comparative deficiency of energy; whilst when the bar is of medium or considerable thickness, the force will be relatively greater. The same rule is applicable to any horizontal lines visible about the writing.

People who have energy, potential power, latent force, write with a heavy forward pressure on their pen, and thus their handwriting takes a progressive "go-a-head" movement.

EXAMPLE.

NAPOLEON BONAPARTE (French soldier; first Consul, and Emperor), 1769–1821. Prominent graphical sign, DESTRUCTIVENESS: denoted by the thickness of the line below the name, &c. A vigorous organisation endowed Napoleon with immense powers, among which were large Calculation, Causality, Comparison, Sublimity, Imitation, Constructiveness, Spirituality, Veneration, Approbativeness, and Combativeness. Conscientiousness was sadly lacking, as can be seen.

10. SECRETIVENESS = *The disposition to conceal; the faculty for hiding; secrecy; evasion.*

Secretiveness has two divisions—

(1) *Reserve* is indicated by the closing of the bodies of the letters *a, d, g, o, q*, &c., at the top; when such letters are left opened, that is, when the return curve does not close, and the letters are not completely "finished off," or really properly formed, the disposition will be a more or less communicative one.

(2) *Policy*, finesse, and tact are indicated by the dwindling or gladiolation of the strokes of which the letters are composed; when the second or third strokes of the letters *n* and *m* are much lower than the first stroke, a relative degree of the quality is implied.

What is more easily conceived than that the impenetrable personality should manifest itself in the

THE MENTAL FACULTIES 99

letters dwindling into a mere filiform line ? Careless, imprudent people write thoughtlessly, and thus omit to close their vowels, &c.

EXAMPLE.

MAXIMILIEN DE ROBESPIERRE (French Revolutionary dictator), 1758–1794. Principal graphical sign, SECRETIVENESS: indicated by the cramped-up aspect of the letters, and their unformed appearance, especially at the end of the name. The law of imperfect curvation is the governing feature of this autograph, and is exemplified in the distorted, irregular shapes of the characters. Self-Esteem, Combativeness, Destructiveness, Acquisitiveness, Eventuality, Individuality, Form, Size, Human Nature, and Cautiousness are largely represented. No want of intellectuality is shown in the separated letters; but, taken as a whole, the facsimile signature is a contemptible, mean, and thoroughly insignificant one, worthy of the tyrant who penned the original. The moral and social faculties are not, generally speaking, well shown up.

11. VITATIVENESS = *The love of life and material enjoyment; the desire to live; tenacity to existence.*

Vitativeness is indicated by the *vigour* apparent in the movement of the writing.

The virile individual drives his pen with a correspondingly forceful sweep of his arm; hence, as a natural consequence, the handwriting produced is more or less bold and forcible.

Persons who are endowed with but little capacity for the enjoyment of life and its pleasures will write a nerveless, feeble style.

EXAMPLE.

THE RIGHT HON. WILLIAM EWART GLADSTONE (orator, statesman, reformer, and classical scholar), 1809–1898. Principal graphical sign, VITATIVENESS: indicated by the vigorous pen-movement. The law of the straight line and square is here prevalent. Language, Form, Individuality, Size, Weight, Colour, Order, Eventuality, Time, Causality, Comparison, Human Nature, Sublimity, Wit, Constructiveness, Benevolence, Hope, Veneration, Firmness, Conscientiousness, Secretiveness, Cautiousness, Approbativeness, Self-esteem, Combativeness, Acquisitiveness, Conjugality, Parental Love, and Amativeness by being all so strongly defined proclaim the autograph to be an extraordinary one.

III.—THE EGOISTIC AND ASPIRING ELEMENTS.

12. APPROBATIVENESS = *Ambition; the desire to shine and receive approval and commendation; love of being thought well of by " Mrs. Grundy."*

Approbativeness has three divisions—
(1) *Ambition and emulation* is shown commensu-

THE MENTAL FACULTIES

rately with the *upward* tendency of the letters and lines of penmanship; when these descend, there will be a relative deficiency of the element.

(2) *The love of display and regard for fashion* is indicated by a curved flourish below the signature; also by the greater or less amount of ornament disposed about the letters generally.

(3) *Sense of character* is shown by the underlining of words, especially of the signature.

Those who love admiration and commendation spontaneously adopt an upward hand, and flourish, as may readily be expected, according to the size of the faculty.

EXAMPLE.

CHRISTOPHER W. VON GLÜCK (German dramatic composer and author). Born, 1714; died, 1787. Conspicuous graphical sign, APPROBATIVENESS: shown by the ornamentation under the surname. The law of the curve and straight line presides over this autograph, wherein the signs for Amativeness, Inhabitiveness, Parental Love, Friendship, Benevolence, Conscientiousness, and Veneration are pre-eminent. Ideality, Sublimity, Imitation, Constructiveness, Wit, Form, Size, Colour, Comparison, Language, Time, Locality, Tune, and Eventuality are highly developed; accounting for the subject's artistic talents.

13. CAUTIOUSNESS = *Prudence ; fear ; sense of danger ; unwillingness to risk anything or trust to " chance ; " anticipation of harm and loss ; wariness ; guardedness.*

Caution has three manifestations—

(1) *Prudence* is revealed by bars or dashes being placed at the endings of sentences, under the signature, beneath paragraphs, &c., and substituted throughout the manuscript for stops. When bars are employed *as well as stops,* the latter being followed by the former, this trait will be large.

(2) *Solicitude* is exhibited by a nervous, agitated style of writing. When large, as a whole the letters will be unfinished, and there will be the want of any advancing motion about the pen-movement; in addition to this, the bars to the *t*'s will terminate, in common with the majority of the finals, abruptly ; and very frequently they will not advance to the right side of the stroke which they are intended to cross.

(3) *Timidity* is manifested more especially by the lack of all *push* in the movement of the handwriting. When large, the stops will be but faintly indicated, and the dots to the *i*'s placed *behind* that letter, &c. Should a stop be used *before* as well as after a letter or phrase, the subject will be particularly fearful. As a whole, the writing signifying a large development of this attribute will be destitute of " go " and " vivacity."

THE MENTAL FACULTIES 103

Careful, watchful people will, as it stands to reason, reveal themselves as such by minding the finishings-off of the letters, and by seeing that the strokes of which their handwriting is composed do not run wildly in all directions or too far.

EXAMPLE.

RICHARD COBDEN (Reformer), 1804–1865. Conspicuous graphical sign, CAUTIOUSNESS: indicated by the stroke below the autograph. Here the straight line and curve are both in evidence as the primary principle of the writing. The signs for Language, Form, Size, Order, Calculation, Causality, Comparison, Ideality, and Constructiveness give a clue as to the subject's first-rate intellectual capacity, which, added to his large Benevolence, Conscientiousness, Firmness, and Combativeness, in addition to large social faculties, made him interested in the welfare of the masses, which caused him to be an initiator of the Free-Trade movement.

14. CONCENTRATIVENESS (CONCENTRATEDNESS OR CONTINUITY) = *Power of application; connectedness; the ability to fix the mind and engage the attention upon whatever is taken up.*

Concentrativeness is indicated in the handwriting by the letters being, as far as possible, connected together, and also by the greater uniformity of their height, and the style.

As the ability to focus the mind depends upon the amount of concentrative power, so the handwriting assumes a concentrated appearance, and the letters, always more or less small, unite themselves neatly together when this faculty is large.

EXAMPLE.

SIR HENRY IRVING (actor and manager; editor of an edition of Shakespeare's works). Born 1838, in England. Principal 'graphical sign, CONCENTRATIVE-NESS: manifested by the uniform height of the letters. Language, Individuality, Size, Weight, Colour, Order, Human Nature, Wit, Benevolence, Conscientiousness, Firmness, Cautiousness, Self-esteem, Executiveness, Friendship, and Amativeness point out, by their development, the direction wherein his greatest strength lies, both as an actor and a gentleman.

15. SELF-ESTEEM = *Proper pride; self-respect; self-reliance; dignity; confidence in one's own powers.*

Self-Esteem has three divisions, the manifestations of which are as follows:—

(1) *Dignity* is indicated by the height at which the *t*'s are barred, or the upper stroke of the capital *P* is placed. When these are set above the upright line which they are intended to cross, the trait will be accordingly well-defined.

(2) *Self-love* is more particularly indicated by curls

THE MENTAL FACULTIES 105

and twists at the commencement or finish of the letters.

(3) *Independence* is manifested in proportion to the height of the capitals and letters generally; and, when the writing is very tall, and the "heads" or first-strokes (or "ascensions") of the letters are inordinately large and "drawn up," this characteristic will be accordingly large.

As Miss Baughan has observed, physiognomists have remarked that pride produces a puffiness of the fibres of the body (hence we say "*puffed* with pride," "*blown* out with a sense of his or her own importance," "*inflated* with haughtiness," and so forth); what is more natural, then, but that the handwriting, which that great physiognomist, Lavater, saw bore a *perfect analogy* to the body, should also assume a puffed appearance? Experience teaches that this is a fact.

EXAMPLE.

WILLIAM II. (Emperor of Germany), born in 1859. Principal graphical sign, SELF-ESTEEM: indicated by the height of the capitals and their exaggerated forms. Language, Individuality, Form, Size, Weight, and Order proclaim the subject to be practical but impulsive, for he lacks judgment. Sublimity, Constructiveness, Imitation, Hope, Conscientiousness, Firmness, Approbativeness, and excessive executive propensities, as well as large Amativeness, Parental Love, Inhabitive-

106   THE LANGUAGE OF HANDWRITING

ness, and Friendship, show the secret nature of this sovereign, whose characters their writer has taken little pains to conceal, as he is lacking in Secretiveness.

IV.—THE MORAL SENTIMENTS.

16. BENEVOLENCE = *Charity ; affection ; tenderness ; the desire to do to others as one would be done by ; kindness of feeling.*

Benevolence has two divisions—

(1) *Sympathy* is indicated by the *inclination* of the handwriting to the *right*. When the letters are upright, or if they take a backward slope, the disposition will be either more self-contained or self-interested.

(2) *Liberality* is denoted by the *flow* of the writing, or outward extension of the terminals and pen-strokes to the right, as a whole.

As the hand of the sympathetic individual is ever *extended towards those who may need its friendly aid*, figuratively speaking and also in reality, so the writing with such a nature will *incline forward*, and thus typify the disposition of the writer ; and in proportion as the disposition is generous so will the finals be extended.

EXAMPLE.

BARONESS BURDETT-COUTTS (philanthropist), born 1814, in England. Principal graphical sign, BENEVO-

THE MENTAL FACULTIES 107

LENCE: shown by the flow of the writing. The law of the straight line and angle governs this autograph. The signs for Love of young and of home, as well as the faculties of Veneration, Conscientiousness, Ideality, and Reason, are all exceedingly well defined; whilst Caution and Executive ability are plainly revealed.

17. CONSCIENTIOUSNESS = *Moral principle; sense of honour and duty; the love of truth and justice.*

Conscientiousness is indicated by *directness* and *straightness* of the strokes of which the handwriting is composed, as well as by the *even* size and *placing* of the letters. When the letters do not run in straight or parallel lines, and are not equidistant, so that the handwriting is oblique or tortuous, the character will not be as honest, sincere, or straightforward as where the letters are placed horizontally, that is, all touching the same plane at their bases (though they need not be, necessarily, rectangularly straight in respect to the paper).

That there is a *directness* of movement with the straightforward person is undoubted; his motives are evident and his motions are straight, to the purpose and without circuitous courses; therefore the handwriting is also even, horizontal, and *straightforward* with such a writer.

EXAMPLE.

GEORGE WASHINGTON (First President of the United States of America), 1732–1799. Dominant graphical sign, CONSCIENTIOUSNESS: denoted by the horizontality and relative parallelism of the strokes. The law of the square, straight line and angle governs this autograph. In it the signs of Firmness, Veneration, Benevolence, Inhabitiveness, Friendship, Parental Love, and Amativeness figure conspicuously; Self-Esteem and Approbativeness being about equally balanced; and Form, Size, Language, and Reasoning capacity very well defined. A beautiful, interesting signature.

18. FIRMNESS = *Will-power; volition; decision; strength of character; steadfastness.*

Firmness has three divisions—

(1) *Power of will* is shown by the form of the terminals and bar to the *t*, &c.; when these end in a bludgeon-like form, and are blunt and thick, the quality will be relatively strong; but when they thin to a point, and no special pressure is exercised by the pen in their formation, the trait will be weaker in proportion.

(2) *Stability* is indicated by a temperate, firm, rectangular, and consistent appearance of the letters; the *t*'s will be barred invariably and regularly, and the letters will be formed after a fixed method.

THE MENTAL FACULTIES 109

(3) *Perseverance* is denoted by the terminals, &c., ending in a hook-shaped manner.

The firm, consistent person has a steady and decisive method of movement; consequently his handwriting is firm and unflinching.

EXAMPLE.

ELLEN TERRY (actress). Born in England, 1848. Conspicuous graphical sign, FIRMNESS: indicated by the decisive, steady style, and blunt terminals, &c. The law of the straight line and curve governs this autograph. In it the signs for Amativeness, Parental Love, Friendship, Inhabitiveness, Benevolence, Hope, Conscientiousness, and Veneration are well defined. Strongly marked, also, are those for Form, Size, Individuality, Human Nature, Constructiveness, Ideality, Comparison, and Imitation. Of Cautiousness and Self-Esteem we have indications in the presence of the bars at the termination of the signature and in the height of the capital letters.

19. HOPE = *Buoyancy; expectation; cheerful anticipation of the future; the inclination to see success in the prospective.*

Hope is indicated by an upward curve of the bars of the *t* at their termination, and also by an upward trend of the final strokes generally. When the latter ascend to an extraordinary extent, there will be the love of speculation and a foolhardy disregard of consequences; whilst when the terminals and crossings to the *t* sink downwards, there will be an absence of cheerfulness, as well as the disinclination to risk anything, and the disposition to look on the dark side of life.

With the melancholy, depressed subject, the body contracts, and the hand imperceptibly droops; but with the buoyant, cheerful individual, the reverse is the case; and the writing is therefore, in this case, of an ascending character. It is a fact that the enterprising individual indites a more expansive hand than the fearful person who is afraid to venture or risk anything. Elasticity of spirit is infallibly shown by the fly-away tendency of the strokes in the handwriting, and the reason for this would seem to be that the gestures of any individual who possesses a cheerful, adventurous mind are of an outward and advancing nature.

EXAMPLE.

WILKIE COLLINS (novelist and dramatist). Born in England, 1824; died, 1889. Conspicuous graphical sign, HOPE: shown by the upward trend of the writing. The law of the straight line and curve governs this autograph. Language, Individuality, Form, Size, Order, Locality, Tune, Eventuality, Human Nature, Reason, Ideality, Sublimity, Imitation, and Constructiveness—all well defined—show

THE MENTAL FACULTIES

us his literary talents; which were augmented by large Benevolence, Veneration, Self-Esteem, Executiveness, Secretiveness, Acquisitiveness, and a strong social nature, such as his handwriting shows him to have possessed.

20. SPIRITUALITY; BELIEF; CREDULOUSNESS; MARVELLOUSNESS OR CREDENCIVENESS = *Trust; impressionability; the inclination to "take for granted" and believe in hearsay; faith.*

This trait is shown by the width or curving of the strokes which form the bases of the letters. People who write in a very pointed fashion, and whose letters narrow to a "*v*"-shaped base, will exhibit less trustfulness than those who indite a *rounded* penmanship.

In youth, when the mind is open and readily impressed, the almost invariable method of writing is "round-hand" or "copy-book" fashion; and, on the contrary, persons who are sceptical adopt a rigid, pointed style of writing. This latter method of forming the letters is often observed with aged people, who think they know everything, and are opinionated.

EXAMPLE.

RICHARD BAXTER (Presbyterian divine and religious writer), 1615–1691. The *curvation* of the strokes gives a clue as to the entire character. The principal graphical sign is SPIRITUALITY : as is demonstrated by the laterally extended bases of the letters. Language, Form, Size, Colour, Comparison, Human Nature, Constructiveness, Ideality, and Sublimity are well indicated ; whilst the signs for Benevolence, Veneration, Conscientiousness, Cautiousness, Combativeness, Acquisitiveness, and Amativeness are all decided. The autographs of the Countess of Huntingdon, Whittier, &c., show Belief to have been very large.

21. VENERATION = *Respect ; modesty ; reverence ; aspiration ; the inclination to pray and exhibit religious feeling.*

Veneration has three manifestations—

(1) *Love of antiquity* is indicated by the shape of the capitals, when they are made according to the " old " pattern [*A*, &c.]

(2) *The love of worship* is denoted according to the positions of the dots above the *i*, the inverted commas (quotation marks), apostrophes, and accents, &c. ; when these are placed *high*, the faculty will be well defined ; when *low*, the reverse will be the case.

(3) *Respect* is shown by simple, homely forms of letters, especially of the capitals.

As humility is the basis of this feeling, it is not surprising to find that those possessed of it should write in an unostentatious, humble way ; which accounts for the " style " being pure and without

THE MENTAL FACULTIES

extravagance. With regard to the height of the dot of the *i*, &c., being said to be indicative of a religious spirit, it must be remembered that the *hand*, as well as the mind and feelings, *trends upwards* as the individual becomes more elevated and high-minded.

EXAMPLE.

J. H. NEWMAN (Cardinal; an originator of the Tractarian movement), 1801–1891. Principal graphical sign, VENERATION : exhibited in the simple and somewhat diminutive capitals, also in the unostentatious forms of the letters generally. The law of the straight line and square governs this autograph. Language, Individuality, Form, Size, Eventuality, Causality, Human Nature, Ideality, Constructiveness, Benevolence, Firmness, and Conscientiousness are amongst the largest intellectual and moral developments. Continuity, Cautiousness, Inhabitiveness, and Friendship are also well represented.

V.—THE PERFECTING OR REFINING GROUP.

22. CONSTRUCTIVENESS = *The faculty for combining and connecting parts; constructive talent; mechanical skill.*

Constructiveness has three divisions—

(1) *Dexterity* is denoted by the method adopted in

uniting the letters and words together; and the more cleverly they are united, the better defined the faculty. For example, when the upstroke of the small d is turned back over the letter and made to do duty for the crossbar of a previously made incomplete t, the aptitude is well exemplified, as it would be, also, were a t to be crossed by (say) the commencement of the letter of another word.

(2) *Ingenuity* is indicated according to the manner in which the characters are united together. When, for example, the initials in the signature of a person are cleverly attached to one another, so that the stroke of one capital letter forms part of another which follows it, the gift will be well represented.

(3) *Contrivance* is indicated according to the greater degree of distinction displayed in forming the letters, particularly the capitals. When these are shaped in an uncommon or original fashion the talent will be proportionately greater than when they are made in an ordinary or unremarkable way.

Quite instinctively, the ingenious individual will have his or her own special method of forming the characters or joining them the one to the other.

It is but natural that he or she should be thus inspired; and the art of writing, considered even from a penman's point of view, offers immense scope for one's resource and ingenuity.

EXAMPLE.

THOMAS ALVA EDISON (inventive genius), born 1847. Principal graphical sign, CONSTRUCTIVENESS: shown by the original types of letters, especially capitals. The law of the straight line, square, and curve is here regnant. Individuality, Form, Size, Weight, Colour, Order, Calculation, Time, Eventuality, Causality, Comparison, Human Nature, Ideality, and Sublimity are all of the first grade, and proclaim a first-class scientific and mechanical mind. Benevolence, Hope, Conscientiousness, Firmness, Veneration, Self-Esteem, Continuity, Combativeness, and Destructiveness are highly developed, and reveal the strong Moral and Executive character for which this famous and excellent man is celebrated.

23. IDEALITY = *Refinement of mind ; imagination ; the sense of perfection.*

Ideality is indicated according to the finish, fineness, and delicacy of the strokes of the handwriting, and also by the letter *e* being formed after the shape of the Greek letter, as well as by the upstroke of the *d* being thrown upward and back over that letter.

It stands to reason that the handwriting of those who possess a sense of perfection should be graceful and delicate, since the movements of such people are always refined and elegant.

EXAMPLE.

H. RIDER HAGGARD (novelist). Born in England in 1856. Conspicuous graphical sign, IDEALITY : shown by the delicate style, looped *d*, &c. The straight line and curve constitute the governing principle of this autograph. Sublimity, Constructiveness, Form, Size, Locality, Individuality, Imitation, Language, Order, Time, Calculation, Eventuality, Comparison, and Causality are well denoted, as well as Human Nature. Self-Esteem and Approbativeness are both clearly defined ; as are Firmness, Conscientiousness, Benevolence, Spirituality, Veneration, and the executive capacities. Of the social and domestic group, Friendship, Inhabitiveness, and Parental Love are noticeable.

24. IMITATION = *The ability to copy and imitate ; to do things after a given pattern ; to work according to a set design ; versatility of talent.*

Imitation has two divisions—

(1) *Mimicry* and the power to copy is indicated by the variability of the size of the letters ; when the dimensions of the handwriting alter according to the size of the paper used, the former becoming larger or smaller as the paper is of greater or less proportions, and if the letters themselves be of unequal sizes, the gift will be correspondingly well defined.

(2) *Assimilation* is manifested by the letters being

THE MENTAL FACULTIES 117

connected *in groups* of (say) three or four letters; some being united together by a *liaison*, and others being left unconnected. This faculty is also said to be shown by a small, quickly-traced, and upward-slanting bar to the letter *t*.

Supple-minded personalities write a somewhat sinuous hand, that is, the letters vary in point of height, for the reason that their natures are, of necessity, plastic and impressionable—capable of assuming diverse phases of character, their many moods causing this variability in the handwriting.

Example.

Paul Gustave Doré (French black-and-white artist, and historical and allegorical painter). Born, 1833; died, 1883. Conspicuous graphical sign, Imitation: revealed by the easily-run-off style. The law of the curve and straight line is here dominant. Form, Size, Colour, Calculation, Individuality, Language, Locality, Reason, Ideality, Sublimity, Constructiveness, and Marvellousness, which are all strongly denoted, contributed toward making this man's genius. Executiveness, Alimentiveness, Acquisitiveness, Inhabitiveness, Friendship, and Approbativeness, are not lacking.

25. MIRTHFULNESS OR WIT = *Sense of the ludicrous; appreciation of the ridiculous; love of humour; the tendency to see the comic side of a situation.*

Mirthfulness is indicated by a waviness of the strokes of which the letters, &c., are composed, and also by a quick, buoyant stroke underneath the signature, &c. When the terminals are thrown off with a sprightly movement, this attribute will be accordingly well developed.

The hand (and, consequently, the *pen*) of the humorous, witty person always has an expressive, buoyant gesture; the mind works quickly, consequently the pen; and the natural result is that the letters are formed in at once the easiest, most rapid, and shortest manner possible.

EXAMPLE.

VICE-ADMIRAL DAVID G. FARRAGUT (American naval officer; distinguished at Mobile), 1801-1870. Notable graphical sign, MIRTHFULNESS: indicated by the wavy final below the autograph. The law which governs this signature is that of the straight line, curve, and square. Parental Love, Inhabitiveness, Friendship, Benevolence, Conscientiousness, Veneration, Firmness, Approbativeness, and Self-Esteem are about equally developed, and all strongly defined. Combativeness, Constructiveness, Imitation, Ideality, Sublimity, Language, Form, Size, Individuality,

THE MENTAL FACULTIES

Locality, Eventuality, and the Reasoning faculties are highly developed. Altogether, a striking piece of calligraphy.

26. SUBLIMITY = *Conception of the vast, stupendous, and magnificent; love of size and quantity; the disposition to consider the whole of things; the inclination to look at and like things on a large scale.*

Sublimity is indicated in proportion to the *size* of the letters and handwriting generally. When the pen-movement is large, the loops being inflated, and the "heads" of the letters assuming exaggerated proportions, this qualification will be relatively large; whereas, when the letters are diminutive, the trait will be proportionately less.

Persons who have *small* hands (which, according to palmists, indicate the love of *size* and vastness) almost invariably write a large style.

EXAMPLE.

CHARLES R. DARWIN (naturalist, discoverer, and author), 1809 – 1882. Conspicuous graphical sign, SUBLIMITY: indicated by the large size of the characters. The law of the straight line, square, and curve governs this autograph. Ideality, Acquisitiveness, Benevolence, Firmness, Conscientiousness, and Friendship, as well as Parental Love, are well defined.

Individuality, Form, Size, Order, Locality, Eventuality, Comparison, and Human Nature are strikingly defined, and give a scientific cast of intellect—rarely equalled, never surpassed.

VI.—THE REFLECTIVE OR REASONING FACULTIES.

27. AGREEABLENESS = *Adaptiveness; adaptability to circumstances; the ability to conform to one's surroundings, and behave suavely, and manifest blandness of manner.*

Agreeableness is manifested by a certain openness of the letters generally, and also by the up-stroke of a letter being carried on with a continuous curve and united with the down-stroke of the same letter, supposing the said letter to be constituted of three or more strokes. For example, where the letter *n* is shaped after the form of a *u*, and the letter *m* takes an inverted form, the trait would be relatively large. This faculty is also indicated by the small letter *r* being formed in the shape of a *u*.

With persons who possess a conciliatory, suave nature, there is a slight undulating and *curved* movement; angles are abolished in the handwriting as far as possible, and round formations to the letters substituted: so it is with the face of persons possessed of this trait, and the *movements* of the subject are ever in agreement therewith.

EXAMPLE.

NATHANIEL HAWTHORNE (American novelist and miscellaneous writer), 1804 – 1864. Conspicuous graphical sign, AGREEABLENESS: indicated by the *u*-shaped *n*'s, &c. Here Language, Form, Size, Eventuality, Reason, Ideality, Sublimity, Wit, and Imitation are well defined, accounting for his literary talents. Benevolence, Hope, Conscientiousness, Spirituality, and Veneration, as well as Executiveness and a sufficient social development, are also implied. Altogether, the embodiment of a highly refined, profoundly interesting, and particularly pleasing personality.

28. CAUSALITY = *The cause-seeking faculty; ability to reason from cause to effect; logical capacity.*

Causality is indicated by the letters being placed singly, *i.e.*, without any connecting strokes between them. It is not difficult to believe that those who meditate and reason much should write in this manner.

The sharp, disconnected pen-movement results in producing the absence of *liaison* which is found to exist with those whose minds are best adapted to trace cause and effect.

EXAMPLE.

FREDERICK HENRY ALEXANDER, BARON VON HUMBOLDT (traveller, German naturalist, scientist, and author). Born, 1769; died, 1859. Conspicuous graphical sign, CAUSALITY: indicated by the letters being placed in juxtaposition, but without connecting lines between them in the majority of cases. The law of the straight line, curve, and sphere governs this autograph. Here the signs for Comparison, Human Nature, Eventuality, Ideality, Sublimity, Constructiveness, Benevolence, Conscientiousness, Hope, Firmness, and Veneration are highly developed; whilst Amativeness, Parental Love, Inhabitiveness, and Friendship are exceedingly well defined. Locality, Language, Individuality, Form, and Size are highly represented. The executive force is well shown in the barred *t*, *H*, and *A*. Acquisitiveness, also, is borne out by the shortened finals, &c. Altogether, an exceedingly masterly, talented, and original production.

29. COMPARISON = *Capacity to compare, contrast, and reason by analogy; inductive reasoning power; lucidity of mind; clearness of mental vision; critical acumen.*

Comparison has two divisions—

(1) *Analysis*, and the ability to classify, is manifested by *clearness* of the handwriting, that is, by the pen-strokes which compose the letters being *distinct* and *unblotted*, no "blind" loops or smeared strokes being observable when the gift is well represented.

THE MENTAL FACULTIES

(2) *Criticism* is indicated by the letters being placed in groups of several letters, *i.e.*, here and there left unconnected.

In order to be able to see clearly mentally, the brain must be unconfused; the handwriting, it will be found, will very quickly indicate whether the ideas are so, or if they are not.

EXAMPLE.

JOHN RUSKIN (philosopher, author, art critic), 1819–1900. Conspicuous graphical sign, COMPARISON: shown by the distinctness of the strokes, &c. The law of the straight line and curve governs this autograph. Eventuality, Ideality, Sublimity, Constructiveness, Imitation, Benevolence, Veneration, Self-Esteem, and Acquisitiveness are well defined; as are Language, Individuality, Size, Form, Order, Time, and Locality also.

30. EVENTUALITY = *Memory of occurrences; recollection of past events.*

Eventuality is indicated by a clearly traced, definite, careful manner of forming the letters; all matters of detail being attended to, and heed being given to the punctuation, &c.

As memory implies that power of the mind which causes things to leave "a deep and lasting impression" in the brain; so, in like manner, the careful

124   THE LANGUAGE OF HANDWRITING

person, who is retentive and systematic, pays attention to his handwriting, forming his letters neatly, finishing them off carefully, and observing all matters of detail with regularity and precision.

EXAMPLE.

E. GIBBON (historian), 1737–1794. Conspicuous graphical sign, EVENTUALITY: indicated by the clear, steady pen-strokes with which the autograph has been traced. Language, Individuality, Form, Size, Weight, Order, Reason, Human Nature, Ideality, Sublimity, and Constructiveness, in addition to Hope, Conscientiousness, Firmness, Self-Esteem, Continuity, Cautiousness, Secretiveness, and Acquisitiveness, are well defined. Friendship is not large, and it is a well-known fact that Gibbon was not fond of society.

31. HUMAN NATURE = *Spontaneous perception of character and motives; sagacity; intuitive judgment.*

Human Nature is indicated by the letters being placed in juxtaposition yet unconnected, and also by the letters, words, and lines of writing being set at equal distances from one another. When the spacing is regular and even, and the letters and words, &c., are so arranged as to occupy the exact extent of the range of the other lines of writing, a straight margin being kept, and no words having to be broken, dashes being placed to fill up the spaces at the end of the sentences to fill up the line, &c., this trait will be large.

Persons who have foresight can, as it were, almost instinctively measure with "the mind's eye" the space which the writing will occupy upon the paper; consequently there will be a sameness and compactness about it.

EXAMPLE.

WILLIAM SHAKESPEARE (dramatist, poet, actor), 1564–1616. Principal graphical sign, HUMAN NATURE: indicated by the separated letters. The law of the curve and straight line is here paramount. All the intellectual faculties, and especially Language, Individuality, Form, Size, Colour, Eventuality, Time, Causality, Comparison, Wit, Imitation, Constructiveness, Ideality, and Sublimity are large. Benevolence is dominant in the moral group, as the gentle style evinces, though Spirituality is large, and Conscientiousness and Hope are by no means deficient. Approbativeness and Self-Esteem are both clearly defined, as are Alimentiveness, Acquisitiveness, Amativeness, and Parental Love.

VII.—THE PERCEPTIVE OR SEEING FACULTIES.

32. CALCULATION = *Mental arithmetic; facility for computing numerically; mathematical talent.*

Calculation is indicated in proportion to the greater clearness and precision visible in the handwriting;

the calmer, more measured, and methodical the style, the stronger will this talent be manifested.

This faculty is peculiar to those who are of the mental and muscular systems; thus, as the style mentioned above is representative of these systems, so it may be considered as indicative of the talent for figures.

EXAMPLE.

FRANÇOIS JEAN DOMINIQUE F. ARAGO (French mathematician, astronomer, and scientist). Born in Spain, 1786; died, 1853. Conspicuous graphical sign, CALCULATION: shown by the careful, precise style. The law of the straight line, curve, and sphere governs this autograph. Conscientiousness, Firmness, Veneration, and Benevolence are exceedingly well defined, as are Approbativeness, Cautiousness, Continuity, Acquisitiveness, Alimentiveness, and the social faculties generally. Individuality, Form, Size, Weight, Colour, Time, Locality, Eventuality, Causality, Comparison, Human Nature, and Constructiveness are all well defined.

33. COLOUR = *Love and perception of colour; sense of shades, tints, hues, and blending colours with taste and discrimination.*

The colour sense is indicated commensurably with the thickness of the up- or down-strokes, and any

THE MENTAL FACULTIES 127

lines which may appear about the handwriting; and when these are dealt out regularly there will be a great knowledge of the effect and love of the beautiful in colour.

Those who possess a full degree of *colour* are vigorous, and have a strong arterial circulation; they throw their whole might into whatever they take up, and on this account write with a proportionately strong pen-movement, producing thick strokes. As these persons have themselves a strong conception of colour, so they are the better adapted to judge and appreciate tints.

EXAMPLE.

PETER PAUL RUBENS (Flemish history painter and diplomatist), 1577–1640. Principal graphical sign, COLOUR: shown by the thick principle of the style generally. The curved plan of the handwriting discloses the subject's artistic genius. Here Amativeness, Friendship, Alimentiveness, Acquisitiveness, and the executive capacities are very much in evidence. Also we find here Form, Size, Weight, Ideality, Sublimity, and Constructiveness. Altogether, the autograph of a highly talented man, if not that of a particularly delicate or ethereal painter.

34. FORM = *Sense of configuration; appreciation for, and recognition of shapes, outlines, and contours.*

Form is shown according to the extent of the symmetry of the letters generally; and the faculty will be particularly large when the capitals are constructed after the plan of the typographic or printed letters. Deformed or ill-shaped and ungraceful, one-sided looking letters, denote a want of this faculty.

Those who appreciate beauty in conformation and outline, will write in a manner which will never prove offensive to the eye.

Grace, symmetry, and simplicity will characterise the tracings of the letters.

EXAMPLE.

ROSA BONHEUR (French animal painter). Born in France, 1822; died, 1899. Conspicuous graphical sign, FORM: indicated by the shapely, well-formed capitals, which resemble the printed letters, as well as by the harmoniously-constructed smalls. The law of the straight line and curve governs this autograph; the pen-tracing of which, being short, yet to the purpose, shows high quality. Size, Weight, Language, Colour, Individuality, Calculation, Order, Eventuality, Locality, and Reasoning Capacity are well defined. Highly developed also we find Human Nature, Ideality, Sublimity, Constructiveness, Imitation, Benevolence, Hope, Self-Esteem, Approbativeness, Acquisitiveness, Alimentiveness, Combativeness, Destructiveness, and Friendship.

THE MENTAL FACULTIES 129

35. INDIVIDUALITY = *Observation ; perception of external and mental objects ; acuteness of apprehension ; the desire to see and identify things.*

Individuality is manifested according to the decisiveness of the strokes of the handwriting, and when the letters, &c., exhibit in parts any *angularity*, and are clearly cut, the faculty will be relatively large. When the finals cease in an angular fashion, and when the up-strokes are pointed and sharply defined, this faculty will be proportionately great. Where " Spirituality " is small, and the letters are pointed at their bases, &c., this quality will be large, because excessive *credenciveness* argues a lack of close observation.

When observation is well defined the writing is more acute, sharp, and decisive, because the writer's ideas with regard to matters in general are also sharp, clear, and distinct. People who write in a confused, muddled style, in which the letters run into one another, or are here and there omitted from the text, are never accurate or clear.

EXAMPLE.

THOMAS H. HUXLEY (biologist and natural scientist), 1825–1895. Principal graphical sign, INDIVIDUALITY: shown by the sharp angularity of the strokes. The law of the straight line, square, and curve governs this autograph. The signs for Language, Form, Size, Weight, Order, Calculation, Time, Locality, Eventuality, Causality, Comparison, Human Nature, Ideality, Sublimity, Benevolence, Conscientiousness, Firmness, Veneration, Self-Esteem, Continuity, Cautiousness, Acquisitiveness, Parental Love, Conjugality, and Friendship shine forth, and proclaim, by their prominence, an equally balanced and exceedingly comprehensive moral and intellectual character.

36. LANGUAGE = *Power of verbal expression; linguistic talent; ability to hold oral communication.*

Language is manifested by the *fluency* of the style, and more especially when the letters, words, and figures, &c., are linked together by a *liaison*. The more rapid, easy, and gliding the movement of the writing, the greater will be the faculty of verbal expression; whilst the more halting, laboured, and slow the style, the less ready will be the writer's flow of words. That the movement of the pen is, as far as possible, commensurate with the flow of the writer's ideas is undoubted.

The reason that the handwriting is fluent, easy, and free with a person who possesses the gift of speech and expression is, that the ideas being rapid and copious, the writer's hand traces the letters continuously, without permitting the pen to leave the paper. Thus, the letters and words are constantly

THE MENTAL FACULTIES

united with a stroke of the pen, and the writing has a gliding movement.

EXAMPLE.

CHARLES DICKENS (novelist), 1812–1870. Conspicuous graphical sign, LANGUAGE: exhibited by the connection of the names. The law of the straight line and curve is here dominant. Very highly developed are Form, Size, Weight, Individuality, Colour, Order, Time, Locality, Eventuality, Comparison, Human Nature, Agreeableness, Imitation, Wit, Constructiveness, and Ideality; as well as Benevolence, along with the domestic and social sentiments, Approbativeness, Executiveness, Alimentiveness, Secretiveness, and Acquisitiveness. An interesting and beautiful autograph.

37. LOCALITY = *Love of travel; desire to see and explore.*

Locality is shown by the manner adopted in forming the letters; and when any outlandish method is employed, the trait will be more or less large accordingly. A zigzag, "lightning" flourish, from the termination of the signature, &c., indicates this faculty to be in a high state of development.

The love of change and variety gives a distaste for those things to which we have been accustomed; consequently, new methods are devised in making the letters. Of course, the possession of this trait does not therefore argue a lack of *Inhabitiveness;* but, as a rule, when "*Locality*" is very large, the desire for a fixed place of abode is not so great as when it is small.

EXAMPLE.

SIR HENRY M. STANLEY, M.P. (African traveller, explorer, and author), 1841. Principal graphical sign, LOCALITY : indicated by the outlandish forms of the *H, S,* and *y,* and especially by their *lengthened* " tails." Language, Individuality, Form, Size, Weight, Time, Eventuality, Sublimity, Constructiveness, Benevolence, Hope, Veneration, Firmness, Approbativeness, and Self-Esteem are all largely represented; whilst the signs for Combativeness, Acquisitiveness, Friendship, Parental Love, and Amativeness are well defined.

38. ORDER = *Sense of method, arrangement, and regularity; appreciation for the motto,* " *There's a place for everything, and everything in its place.*"

Order is shown by all stops, crossings to *t's* (provided that the barred type of the letter be habitually used), and matters of detail generally being attended to ; when the letters are not merely neatly finished off, but *extra strokes* are added to them, in order to give them a more neat and perfect appearance, the writer will be of a fussy, over-methodical nature.

THE MENTAL FACULTIES   133

The orderly person is particular over small matters —the veriest trifles, the merest details; none escapes his attention. Therefore, as such is the case, what is more common-sense than to find the stops and extra strokes all placed carefully by the writer possessed of the faculty?

EXAMPLE.

THOMAS HARDY (novelist). Born 1840. Conspicuous graphical sign, ORDER: indicated by the stop placed after the names, and the carefully traced "hand." Language, Individuality, Form, Size, Weight, Colour, Time, Reason, Eventuality, Intuition, Ideality, Constructiveness, Conscientiousness, Firmness, and Veneration are all exceedingly well defined. Cautiousness, Continuity, Executiveness, Acquisitiveness, and Parental Love, as well as Amativeness, are also highly developed or extremely active in this talented man's organism, hence well shown up in the autograph.

39. SIZE = *Cognisance of size; ability to determine the dimensions of objects, and discern whether one part is in proportion to another, &c.; sense of perspective and the fitness of things.*

Size is denoted by the relative proportions of the capitals as regards the smalls. When their respective sizes are in keeping with each other, the faculty will be better defined than when either is so large or so small as to look out of place. Strictly speaking, the capitals should be about twice the size of the bodies of the small letters. When the faculty is large, the strokes of the letters will be parallel and the lines of writing will be equidistant, even, and placed in a correct position upon the paper.

As is to be expected, persons with a keen sense of the fitness and adaptation of parts observe a strict sense of uniformity between the size of the respective letters.

EXAMPLE.

J. M. W. TURNER (subject and landscape painter), 1775–1851. Conspicuous graphical sign, SIZE: shown by the proportion between the large and small letters. Individuality, Form, Weight, Colour, Reason, Human Nature, Sublimity, and Imitation are all well defined, and assisted his artistic efforts. Firmness, Self-Esteem, Executiveness, Acquisitiveness, Vitativeness, and Amativeness are all represented in varying degrees.

40. TIME = *Sense of the duration and lapse of time; the ability to comprehend the laws of time, and understand metre and rhythm.*

Time is shown according to the unity and regularity of the pen-movement; and when the letters are placed harmoniously and methodically the trait will be well defined; whilst when they are set in a

THE MENTAL FACULTIES

higgledy-piggledy fashion, and the strokes are not arranged evenly, there will be less of the quality.

The very movements of a punctual person are methodical and regular; notice the step of the soldier, who is obliged to be so; the motion of the hand of persons who possess this trait in a high degree is therefore consistent, and, as a matter of course, the handwriting is likewise regular.

EXAMPLE.

SIR ISAAC NEWTON (physicist, discoverer, natural philosopher; demonstrated the law of gravity). Born in England, 1759–1808. Conspicuous graphical sign, TIME: indicated by the even systematic flow of the "style." The law of the straight line, square, and sphere governs this autograph. Conscientiousness, Firmness, Veneration, Calculation, Benevolence, Order, Form, and Size, therefore, are well defined; as are also Individuality, Weight, Language, Locality, Eventuality, Reason, Sublimity, Ideality, and Constructiveness. Parental Love, Inhabitiveness, and Friendship are conspicuous; whilst Acquisitiveness is well represented.

41. TUNE = *Love of melody, musical ability, sense of tone, the ability to appreciate concord, modulation, and harmony.*

Tune is indicated by the *tout-ensemble* of the handwriting, and the softer and more delicate the "touch" of the pen, and the more gliding the strokes of which the letters are composed, the stronger will the gift be defined.

Music is inherent in the vital system, and pertains to those persons who are susceptible and tender-hearted; thus, as the writing of these individuals is soft and in accord with their nature, so may this style be considered as significant of the gift. The expression of the gift of Tune is dependent upon the action of the muscular system; and when this is well defined the fingers, &c., taper, which facilitates a curvilinear penmanship.

EXAMPLE.

GEORGE FREDERIC HANDEL (German composer and organist), 1685–1759. Principal graphical sign, TUNE: illustrated by the outward curvature of the up-and-down strokes. Form, Size, Weight, Colour, Order, Tune, Comparison, Causality, Sublimity, Ideality, and Constructiveness are all well defined, and together indicate the phase of mentality required to produce the works of this eminent musician. Benevolence, Conscientiousness, Marvellousness, and Veneration, as well as Self-Esteem, Executiveness, Acquisitiveness, Alimentiveness, Inhabitiveness, and Amativeness are all exceedingly conspicuous, and assisted the creative genius of Handel, as well as adding to the efficiency of his moral and social nature.

42. WEIGHT = *Ability to balance oneself and remain in a perpendicular position; the power to maintain one's equilibrium; sense of the laws of gravity, force, and resistance.*

Weight is shown according to the relative positions of the individual letters, &c.; and when they slope evenly in the same direction, and the penmanship is written with a steady, consistent pressure upon the pen, so that the writing is set compactly, the faculty will be proportionately large; whereas, when the handwriting is set straggling in all directions, some letters slanting to the left, others standing vertically, and others sloping again to the right, and the pressure of the pen is unequal, sometimes heavy and at others light, the faculty will be relatively weak.

Control over the *muscular system* must engender control over the movement of the hand; therefore, the stronger the sense of *weight*, the firmer, more decided, and less shaky the writing.

EXAMPLE.

SIR J. EDGAR BOEHM (Anglo-Hungarian sculptor). Born, 1834; died, 1890. Prominent graphical sign, WEIGHT: indicated by the compactly-turned, well-adjusted pen-strokes. The law of the straight line, curve, and square dominates this autograph. Hence we find the signs for Language, Individuality, Form, Size, Colour, Order, Time, Locality, Comparison,

Eventuality, Sublimity, Ideality, and Constructiveness all exceedingly well defined; whilst those for Benevolence, Hope, Conscientiousness, Firmness, Veneration, Self-esteem, Approbativeness, Continuity, and Cautiousness are more or less conspicuous. The Executive capacity is marked by the line underneath the names, and Acquisitiveness, Friendship, and Amativeness are revealed.

X.

DELINEATING

AND now a word or two remains to be said respecting the practical application of graphology.

Having a suitable handwriting specimen before us (as described in that section of this work devoted to the discussion of the materials necessary to the proper practising of the science), the first thing to be done is to determine the *quality* of the writer's organisation— the calibre of his mind; and, for this purpose, we must observe the general aspect of the writing, the grace, finish, and symmetry, or otherwise, of the pen-strokes, &c.

This being decided upon, the size and form of the letters come next for our attention. If the writing be *large*, there will be power, because, provided that all else is equal, *size* implies strength and scope of mind; if *small*, the reverse. As regards the shape of the lines by which the writing is bounded, we must have recourse to the fundamental elements of *Form;* but, as there are two great divisions or classes of writing, viz., *straight* or *curved*, it will be sufficient if we, in the first place, consider whether the strokes take a (1) *rounded* or (2) *rectilinear* course, when we shall decide accordingly upon the writer possessing, either (1) rectitude, order, logic, cogitative powers, conscientiousness, and a masculine, scientific cast of mind; or else, (2) intuition, benevolence, comparison, idealism, and a feminine mind, with oratorical, histrionic, or musical tastes or talents. In the former case the writer will be conservative; in the latter, enthusiastic, emotional, and affectionate.

This being settled, we shall have gained some knowledge of the subject's temperament, for those of the motive system write angularly, or with square-shaped characters; whilst such as are of the vital system pen a spherical or ovoid " hand." As the mental system enters into the subject's composition, so will the basic forms created by the other two primary systems become the less distinct. Supposing that the choosing of the ink and paper used be left to the writer's own discretion, that which is selected is very indicative of temperament.

Those, for example, of the vital system will prefer either red or pale tints—bluish, greenish, or purple; those of the motive will adopt black; while those of the mental system will rather have mixed shades of colour than anything else.

As a rule, fancy or ornamented notepaper will denote caprice or affectation, though it may indicate the mere "follower of fashion." The *texture* or consistency of the paper, of course, as well as the appear-

DELINEATING

ance of the ink upon it, will tell of the writer's *environment;* that is to say, a rich person will be likely to utilise a thicker and more costly notepaper on which to write, also better ink, than a poor individual.

When the letter containing the form of application to the graphologist is submitted by post, the envelope which would be used then gives some clue as to the writer's character; the method of putting on the stamp being particularly pregnant with meaning.

If the stamp be affixed carefully, it would denote order, prudence, and carefulness; whilst should it be fastened on hurriedly and placed in a crooked position, it would then show haste, impulse, and impressionability, and so on. The same rules apply to the *directing of the envelope,* of course, as to the body of the MS.

The *proportion* of the strokes will have to come in for the next share of attention, and care must be taken to see how they harmonise one with another. After which, the degree of personal activity (length of strokes) and excitability (sharpness of strokes) must be gauged. The best plan to follow then is to observe which graphological signs strike one most, and then to bear in mind what such signs represent. By taking, in this way, the leading traits and balancing one against another, graphology is practised *scientifically.*

It should be observed, that when a special graphic sign is marked *only here and there,* the manifestation of the quality of which· such a sign is representative will be of a transitory, intermittent, or fluctuating description. The *signature* must be, in all cases, the " final court of appeal," for it will denote the *latent* powers of the subject, the inherent disposition, and what the individual is capable of becoming.

XI.

ELEMENTARY STUDIES

1. JUSTIN M'CARTHY, M.P.,
Irish Politician, Novelist, and Littérateur.

With Kind Regards,
Very truly Yours,
Justin Mc Carthy.

THIS autograph, the letters of which are small, carefully finished, often unconnected, and with well-minded stops, shows capacity for detail, a love of particularising rather than of generalising or making sweeping statements, great love of perfection and finish, good taste, and excellent intellectual development.

Notice the short terminals, the prudence of the writer, how particular he is. Remark, further, how low down the vertical line the *t* is "crossed," indicating that self-government has been practised, and denoting a habitual dislike of rule or domineering.

2. CLIFFORD HARRISON,

Reciter, Author, &c.

A strongly individualised autograph. Originality of method is visible in the whole outline, in the uncommon forms of the capitals, the pear-shaped dot to the *i*, and the somewhat square-looking style. Artistic perception is shown in the beautifully rounded sweep of the *l*; whilst imagination, lucidity of mind, and conception of character are shown in the exaggerated proportions of the *C* and the absence of any connecting links between many of the letters. Notice the sense of perfection, shown by, among other things, the bar put across the top of the *H* to make the letter the more finished in appearance. Mr. Harrison, therefore, does not believe that he has yet learned all there is to be learned about his art; he aims high; caution, thoroughness in work, and perseverance— indicated, respectively, by the dots to the *i* being placed just over the letter and the stop put after the names, the evenness of the letters, and the hook-like final to the crossing of the *H*, are strong points in

ELEMENTARY STUDIES 145

this gentleman's character, and contribute, in no small degree, to his success.

3. MARION TERRY,
Actress.

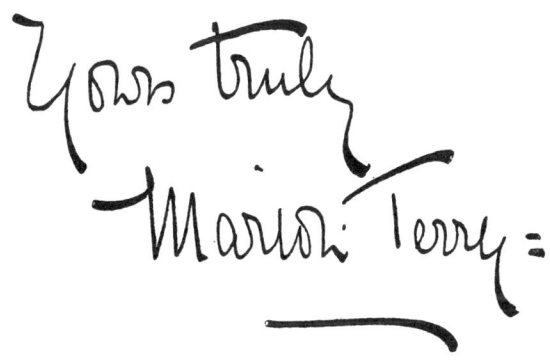

The above autograph, by its *simple*, yet very unconventional strokes, suggests extraordinary abilities of many kinds. The grace of the letters suggests artistic talents; and their original forms, marked individuality.

The writing of this lady is, itself, light and delicate; yet the lines which surmount the capitals, and that which underlines the signature, show a great love of beauty and all things that appeal to the senses, such as music, flowers, and so forth. Vivid imagination is shown by the capitals being set apart from the rest of the letters, together with æsthetic judgment and desire for finish in all things.

There is great force of will in the heavy terminals and soaring *t*-crossing; but considerable caution in the *i*-dot flying *behind* the letter, as well as in the presence of those bars at the end of the signature.

4. FLORENCE MARRYAT,
Novelist.

An autograph composed of large-sized characters, and exhibiting a pronounced movement and continuous connection of the letters, consequently indicative of a vivid imagination, much impressionability, and literary and elocutionary ability.

The mind of this clever writer is quick and bright; [she is evidently capable of producing at considerable speed, under pressure. At the same time, notice the desire for finish in the marks between the lines under the names: observe the double-barred *F*.

There is impulse, activity, and energy shown, by the forward motion of the writing, the ascendant style, and the strongly marked lines across the *F* and below the signature.

In the slope, wide curves, and well spaced-out

letters we have the signs not only of affection, kindliness, and sociability, but also of musical talents. The tall capitals suggest, as do also the high letters generally, self-respect: there is no flinching from undertaking difficult tasks.

5. CYRIL MAUDE,
Actor.

The letters of which this autograph is composed have been traced with a comparatively small expenditure of nerve-force, the pen-movement being to the purpose, unstudied, non-complicated, and rapid, and many of the up and down strokes being formed by single straight strokes; showing an organisation of high quality, possessed of considerable mental activity, acuteness, and, withal, simplicity of nature.

The small size of the letters shows what may be termed the "microscopic" faculty, *i.e.*, that one which magnifies the importance of things and gives consideration to detail; and the *perfectly* curved, cultivated style indicates how well trained are the writer's artistic tastes. Without going into these in detail, we may remark the imagination and humour evidenced by the prolonged commencement of the *M*.

There is not much "paradoxicalness" revealed, as the letters are all united; but, rather, an available, utilitarian cast of intellect.

6. EMIL SAUER,
Pianist, Composer, &c.

An autograph composed of elegant and graceful pen-strokes; indicating a well-trained and thoroughly cultivated *artistic* sense. The almost *circular* lines reveal the subject's musical capacity, and the *regular motion* of the writing his powerful sense of rhythm. Herr Sauer's power as an executant proceeds largely from his well-defined sense of Touch and Balance, or Resistance; shown by the equality of the slope of the letters, and the regularity of pressure which has obviously been expended in forming them.

In the mount of the signature, as well as in the strongly-traced pen-sweep from right to left and back again, we see the signs for ambitiousness and assertion, which serve to help him win his way in the public's estimation.

7. CHARLES BERTRAM,
Prestigiator.

Yours faithfully
Charles Bertram

The autograph reproduced herewith gives evidence of great dexterity and adaptability by its easy, running style; also a powerful social nature and hospitality, a strong incentive to entertain and amuse others, by the wide spacing out of the letters.

"Weight," which gives the conjurer facility of manipulation and the ability to use his fingers with ease and sureness, is indicated mainly by the regular slant of the letters, their perfect parallelism.

The united names indicate the gift of speech, which a magician should never be without; and the *u*-shaped *r*'s and *m* show, the adaptability so necessary to ensure success and bring him *en rapport* with his audience.

150   THE LANGUAGE OF HANDWRITING

8. CISSIE LOFTUS,

Mimic, Actress, Authoress, &c.

[signature: Yours Sincerely Cissie Loftus]

A thoroughly legible, individualised, scriptory declaration, indicative (by virtue of its almost perfect curves and corroborative signs of mental cultivation) of æsthetic tastes and artistic perceptions.

There has not, up to the present time, been any sign located in the handwriting as indicative, *per se*, of imitative ability; but this expressive and readily-turned-out pen-gesture shows many of the qualifications which would go a long way towards ensuring such.

The height of the capitals gives self-valuation; hence Miss Cissie Loftus has not only given evidence of her innate dramatic talent, but has also commanded a leading position, although so young, for some time past in the dramatic world.

9. JOHN BURNS, L.C.C., M.P.,
Labour Representative.

[handwritten: I send you by this post what you require. Yours truly, John Burns]

An autograph comprised of straightforwardly-turned strokes; hence expressive of *directness* in action, of speech, and everything else.

The united names give power *to speak;* and the angular forms of the letters immense perseverance, energy, and force of character.

Practical, rather than theoretical (letters joined together), our subject has ever in view what he thinks will be of advantage to the multitude.

There is less suavity about Mr. Burns than there

is about many people, and far less deference or humility. He would not "mince matters."

By a careful inspection of *each* of the graphical signs embodied in the above autograph, an excellent and correct estimate of the man can be made.

10. JOSEPH PARKER, D.D.,
Preacher.

An autograph, formed of a series of extravagant, defiant, and unconventional pen-strokes, expressive of great individuality, independence of opinion, and fearlessness of spirit.

Power of words, of a vigorous and forcible nature, is indicated by the attached names; and this faculty, being, as it is, associated with an intense love of the sublime and infinite (large handwriting), gives an oratorical temperament.

Observe the *two* advancing lines under the names, also the tremendous sweep of the *P*, indicative of courage, self-valuation, and aggression. Dr. Parker was "built" to lead, direct, and organise, not to sit down calmly and pray whilst another did the work.

For the contemplative, meek, and mild Christian we must look elsewhere.

11. SIR GEORGE NEWNES, Bart., M.P.,
Founder of George Newnes, Ltd.

An autograph expressive, not only of literary talent of a pronounced type, but also of great clearness of mind, straightforwardness of principle, and enterprise. There are business habits shown.

Remark the colon placed after the abbreviation, "Geo.," of the Christian name, and the full stop at the end of the surname.

Executiveness (strongly-marked advancing terminal of *G*), judgment (temperate style, letters mostly united), and refinement (delicate strokes), are all strong points in Sir George's "make-up," and serve to show the means whereby he has succeeded in life.

12. ALFRED RUSSEL WALLACE, F.R.S., &c.,
Scientist.

Yours very truly
Alfred R. Wallace

This interesting specimen indicates fine mental capacity, for the strokes of which it is composed are (1) clear, and (2) definite.

The somewhat acute forms of the capitals show the investigating mind of the scientist, whilst the connection of the letters denotes the practical cast of intellect so necessary to ensure one's labours being of utility.

There is extreme cultivation shown by the elegance of the characters, and no lack of imagination (curved, light, and flyaway style). Order is present in the stop placed after the *R*. Constructive talents are revealed by the singular method of forming the letter *R*.

The defensive-aggressive flourish indicates the power of pushing forward the theories that have made this eminent man's name so famous.

13. LORD LEIGHTON, P.R.A.,

Painter, &c.

Who, after studying scientific graphology, could mistake this writing for aught but that of an artist? Observe the curvilinear plan upon which it is constructed, and by which we gain a clue as to the writer's bias.

Originality of design, a great sense of form, proportion, and colour, extreme refinement of mind, and a vivid imagination, are all shown (by the unconventionality, elegance, symmetry, thickness of the *F* head and *L* base, delicacy, and movement of the writing). The names, by being united, show the eloquence for which Lord Leighton gained a great reputation.

156   THE LANGUAGE OF HANDWRITING

14. LADY HENRY SOMERSET,
Philanthropist, &c.

This autograph expresses Lady Henry Somerset's large-heartedness, her generosity, wide sympathies, and power of organisation, in the large size of the letters, also by their right-handed inclination, &c.

Independence of character (highly-barred *t*), added to a strong degree of assertion (defensive aggressive terminal), give Lady Henry Somerset the desire to pursue a public career.

Her power of speaking, for which she became famous, is indicated by, among other things, the united names.

15. GEORGE ROBERT SIMS ("Dagonet"),
Novelist, Journalist, Poet, &c.

An autograph indicative of much literary talent, as the attachment of the letters (showing facility of

expression), the wavy, expansive style (denoting wit
and humour), and the cultured, curvilinear outlines of
the strokes (indicating imagination), respectively show.
The *practical* cast of the writer's mind (constantly
united characters) indicates that he would deal, principally, with the life, manners, habits, and customs
about him, rather than with the intangible or ethereal.
The marked slant of the writing to the right denotes
the *strongly-feeling* nature which all those who are
acquainted with this most popular writer's works
would expect to figure prominently in his compositions; whilst the lasso-like flourish under the signature indicates the defensive, attacking spirit which
has always caused him to stick up for the poor and
oppressed.

16. Sir W. H. Russell,

War Correspondent.

A highly significant and very typical example.
Who, but a person of extreme mental force, could

have traced the bold, wide, and rather rigid strokes of which this autograph is composed? The defensive, courageous terminal suggests the brave spirit requisite for the war correspondent, and the writer's literary talent is implied by the qualities shown by the connected capitals and the general look of culture apparent in the specimen. Stops are placed after the initials *W* and *H*, indicating a certain attention to detail; but the autograph as a whole indicates ardour, aspiration, self-reliance, and a progressive grade of mentality.

17. SYDNEY GRUNDY,

Playwright, &c.

This compact autograph, with its carefully constructed letters, and duly placed stop at the termination thereof, suggests "infinite capacity for taking pains," and for persevering with what is taken up.

Nor are the signs which imply Mr. Grundy's literary talents absent. The shortly-turned, definite strokes, which do duty for the letters, also the looped-back *d*, show the well educated, trained mind. Many of the characters are placed singly, side-by-side, telling of creative skill, insight into human nature, discriminating ability, and many similar traits necessary to the dramatist.

There is power for minute observation in the angularly-formed letters, and no lack of ability for putting thoughts into words, judging from the G being connected with the r, and the d to the following letters.

XII.

ADVANCED STUDIES

Mr. George Alexander.

IN this autograph the principal features which we notice are its expansive and rapid movement, along with the curtailed final strokes to the letters.

Mental, rather than physical, energy and activity are typified by the relatively long up-strokes and short " tails."

The small size of the writing and somewhat angular style will give capacity for detail and minute observation; whilst the presence of the dots after the names shows power of laying out his plans according to method, attentive and careful habits.

Mr. Alexander is practical, eminently so; all the letters in the signature are run on to each other; he

ADVANCED STUDIES

is well adapted to understand the technique of his art; and, besides possessing (as we shall presently see) all the important qualifications for being, himself, an excellent actor, should understand the application of principles, and have excellent judgment in respect to the absolute requirements of the stage.

Caution and prudence are to be seen in the short terminals and underlined names; also power of will.

The ascendant style will give ambition, but the drooping finals and compression noticeable in the handwriting will make the nature the reverse of particularly hopeful and somewhat self-conscious. Imagination is suggested in many ways, and not least by the wildly extravagant form of the *d* where that letter unites with the *e* in the surname, and this denotes also *verve,* and an ardent, enthusiastic temperament.

There is power of language in the united letters; but the instinct for realising character (shown by the separation of the characters) is not as clearly shown in the signature as in the rest of the writing of our subject. Mr. Alexander's methods are revealed by the specimen before us, however, in an unmistakably plain manner, and perhaps the one great point so conspicuous in this popular actor-manager's mode of treatment, is his quiet, unobtrusive manner, indicated conjointly by the "retiring" aspect of the letters at the ends of the names and the simple forms of the capitals.

SIR LAWRENCE ALMA-TADEMA, R.A.

Variety is charming, and herewith is given the signature of Sir L. Alma-Tadema, R.A., the well-known artist. It forms an interesting study. The handwriting is minute—in fact so small that, in order to thoroughly appreciate it, one needs to use a powerful reading-glass, in order to dissect the various graphic signs which are present in it.

When we come to examine it closely, we observe that it is a rather nervously-traced, and very delicate piece of handwriting, the strokes of which it is composed being to the purpose, yet somewhat irregular—sharp at times, and frequently agitated. These data index corresponding conditions of mind. There is an immense amount of susceptibility shown, as well as impulse, refinement of organisation, and tone of mind. Such fine, slender pen-strokes at once proclaim superior

organic quality. I never saw a person whose mind was of a low order write in this manner, and I don't suppose any of my readers have either.

Now that we have noted the general aspect of the strokes, what next commands our attention is the elegance of the style. It will be perceived that loops, or circular pen-movements, are used in the formation of the letters. The reason for this is not far to seek. The curve is emblematic of Art. Persons whose bodies are constructed after a curvilineal principle, and whose features constitute a series of curved lines, are the best able to reproduce curved patterns. It has been said that there is no such thing as a straight line in nature, and nature, all will admit, is essentially Art.

Well, the flowing curves in this autograph at once testify to the artistic tastes of the writer, and now that we have premised this much we will proceed to investigate the separate graphological signs.

Our subject being as he is a painter, we naturally expect to find a large development of the organs of Form, Size, and Colour, as well as of Ideality and Constructiveness. We shall not be disappointed. The elegant shapes of the letters imply perception of beauty in contour and outline; their regular dimensions and placing denote Size—the sense of proportion and perspective; and the alternate fairly dark strokes signify Colour, whilst the refinement of style and the connected letters respectively indicate large Ideality and Constructiveness.

The autograph, by the small size of the letters, shows capacity for detail—great attention to minutiæ and matters of comparatively " small importance," as they are termed. With such a high degree of the artistic faculties then, we may infer great sense of perfection, much love of intricate work and exactness. Evidently Sublimity— which gives appreciation for and conception of the vast, boundless, and stupendous—is smaller than Individuality (rather sharp " turn strokes " to letters).

Other qualities which are well represented are Combativeness (advancing line below autograph), Secretiveness (letters inclined to dwindle into a thread-like line), Continuity (all letters united, small handwriting, calm, steady style), and Conscientiousness (letters placed evenly, and all running in a level line), which together assist in making him painstaking, persevering, and capable of executing his designs.

The letters, by being placed well apart, typify a gracious friendly nature, and the looped *A* and *L*, &c., denote a full development of Philoprogenitiveness—affection for children.

Sir Squire Bancroft.

Sir Squire Bancroft, whose signature is reproduced herewith by his kind permission, has a particularly interesting personality, which is well indicated by the graphological signs which we are about to consider.

His handwriting, we notice, is (1) graceful; (2) cultivated—not in any degree approaching "copperplate" or round-hand—without either *vulgar* or *extravagant* pen-movements; and (3) has been very quickly delineated, and traced upon the paper. And these facts assure us that the organic quality and

ADVANCED STUDIES 165

mental grade of Sir Squire Bancroft is high; also, that he has a quick intelligence, and excellent powers of comprehension. His *artistic* capacity is illustrated in the curved formations of many of the letters, notably of the *S*, *q*, *e*, *B*, and *a*.

The perceptive powers preponderate—as the signs for Individuality (acute, definite outlines to most of the letters), Form (compact, elegant shapes to capitals), Size (margin—of letter—even, lines and letters equidistant), Weight (equality in slant of letters), Order (*i* dotted, stop placed after signature), Language

(*very* fluent style, names joined), and Time (even, regular flow in motion of handwriting, &c.,) which are larger than those for either Causality or Comparison (capital letters not united with the rest, and but few unconnected, in signature) indicate.

Hence our subject will be noted for his ability to observe correctly—to note the outlines, contours, bulk, and magnitude of objects—to perceive and apprehend the laws of gravity and motion—to notice whether things are put in their proper places and himself to pay attention to the law of order. Form and Size, too, give the capacity to picture in the mind's eye the character portrayed and a sense of fitness—both necessary in dramatic representation — while Sir Squire Bancroft's large Language—added to his well-defined Comparison, large Human Nature (letters often unconnected in body of letter, besides being often of angular forms, and nearly always at equal distances apart), very strongly indicated Wit (brisk, hasty, and buoyant movement of writing), exceedingly influential Ideality (refined style, *e* Greek-shaped, final of *d* usually turned back or over letter, among numerous other signs), well-represented Sublimity (rather large letters of handwriting), and Agreeableness (*u*-shaped *n*), shows us, in an unmistakably plain manner, the source from whence histrionic talents are mainly derived.

His fine sense of humour, tempered by deliberation and judicious restraint (shown by the temperate final strokes), in combination with taste, imagination, power of "sensing" character, lucidity of intellect, and the faculty for interesting and amusing others spontaneously, reveal at once the leading gifts of Sir Squire Bancroft.

As regards his other characteristics—which are numerous, on account of the interesting developments and combinations of the organs—it may be observed that a good degree of Force, Executiveness, and Resistance (shown by the thick bar to the *t* and the strongly marked line which sweeps to the left under the autograph) coupled with large or full Firmness (blunt terminals), Conscientiousness (letters set running in a level-line—non-complicated strokes, &c.), Continuity (names, and words often—united—unmistakable signs of thoroughness—not much variability in methods employed in forming letters), and Ambition (ascendant lines of writing) gives, to a great extent, the incentive to utilise his endowments to advantage.

In the slope of the writing, moreover, and in the very wide spaces between the letters (they are more crowded in the signature than in the rest of the specimen of handwriting), we are shown the signs for Benevolence and Friendship, which, giving a generous, kindly instinct, tell us that Sir Squire Bancroft has others besides himself whom he desires to befriend; and this, I think, has been fully demonstrated in his thoughtful and liberal aid on behalf of the hospitals.

MR. WILSON BARRETT.

In this case the letters are placed singly, the strokes being small, sharp, and endorsed with considerable "life," if the term may be allowed in connection with the matter in hand; these facts

168 THE LANGUAGE OF HANDWRITING

indicate a predominance of the mental system, that is, a powerful development of the anterior or intellectual lobes of the brain. But, in addition to this, the thickness of the writing gives evidence of the vital elements being well defined, whilst the concentrated look of the letters generally assures us that there is, as well, a good degree of the motive temperament. Hence, as we find from the simple, direct strokes which compose the letters, that the organic quality is high, we have by the above combination of the three systems, a vigorous organisation, which gives power, and, with specific signs to be presently enumerated, signal abilities.

Excitability is determined by sharpness, and there is sufficient of this condition to render our subject susceptible and impressionable, as can be seen from the acute terminal below the small *t*'s.

Activity is denoted by length. The letters in the signature are not particularly long. What strikes us about this autograph at first sight is its thickness. Yet we notice at the same time that the strokes are temperate and well-controlled.

The heavy down strokes denote Amativeness as well as Force-energy. This quality is supplemented in the first place by a strong colour sense, shown by the heavy stroke which crosses the *t*'s. and again by large Destructiveness, which is indicated by the black line which is traced under the name.

Secretiveness, which no good actor can afford to be

without in a marked degree, is plainly shown by the tightly closed *o* in "Wilson," whilst Combativeness is conspicuous in the advancing line drawn below the signature.

Now, all these qualifications which tend to give force and expressiveness, if well backed up by a powerful intellect, as they are in this instance, are indispensable to any exponent of the dramatic art who essays to play such *rôles* as those assumed by our subject.

But now we come to consider the development of the intellectual faculties. Of these Form (elegant capitals), Individuality (distinct pen strokes), and Size (capitals and small letters well adapted to each other in point of size), besides Language (flowing pen strokes), Comparison (letters mostly set side by side and unconnected), Human Nature (letters equidistant), and Ideality (original and symmetrically-shaped letters) are, perhaps, the most prominent.

Of the moral sentiments we may observe that Veneration is evidently active, as is signified by the altitude at which the *i* is dotted. This faculty must needs be in some measure called into play when writing or playing such a part as "Marcus Superbus," unless a person be one of those who profess never to feel any emotions they portray.

Approbativeness, as evidenced by the ascending motions of the letters and flourish, is larger than Self-esteem, the capitals being by no means tall.

The letters are not set far enough apart to suggest a full degree of Friendship.

Mr. Barrett's ambition is not merely to mix in society and "go out in the world," but the curious loop which twists to the left, uniting the two upright strokes of the *t*'s together, tells us that he must have a large corner in his heart for children— Parental Love being thereby indicated in a marked degree.

These faculties constitute those which are the best defined, and although space does not permit a full analysis of this interesting gentleman's character, it may be mentioned that the signature differs from the rest of the handwriting specimen, inasmuch as in the latter the letters are mostly *united*, whereas in the former the opposite is the case.

MR. RUTLAND BARRINGTON.

In this specimen there are signs of a truly artistic temperament revealed. How beautifully *curved* are each and every stroke; and how graceful is the whole

ADVANCED STUDIES 171

autograph. The faculties of Language (names united by running stroke of pen), Constructiveness (*t* barred by crossing which becomes commencement of *B*), Ideality (perfect curves and symmetrical style), Wit (buoyant strokes—especially in *R*, *B*, and at the end of the surname), Agreeableness (*u*-shaped *n*), and Human Nature (even spaces kept between letters— one or two of which latter are unjoined), assist to give dramatic abilities, and are here all well represented. It is to these qualities that Mr. Barrington owes his originality, refinement, humour, power to interest and engage the attention of his listeners, and his artistic judgment of character.

In the tendency which is shown—unfortunately not in the mere signature alone, which is given— to vary the size of the handwriting, according to the dimensions of the paper used, we have the sign for Imitation: but this faculty is not so prominent as those previously mentioned; which combine to give him a marked individuality of method, so conspicuous in this talented actor. Time and Tune, which give musical talents (melody and harmony) are shown by the very *round* shapes of most of the letters and their regular motion.

Mr. Barrington has an excellent eye for form and colour both—as can be seen from the pure forms of the capitals and their alternating dark and light strokes. Approbativeness is indicated by the ascendant type of autograph, and by the flourish below

172 THE LANGUAGE OF HANDWRITING

the names; this faculty giving the desire to be appreciated, hence adding to his dramatic capabilities.

Other characteristics which are developed are Sympathy (in the soft, sloping, outspread strokes of which the letters are composed), and Friendship (letters set far apart), which together make him kind-hearted and companionable; while Combativeness,—which is denoted by the sweeping stroke from the *t*—more particularly at the termination of the signature,—adds executive capacity and the power of making up the mind.

Altogether, this autograph is a most interesting example, and will well repay closer inspection.

Mr. Max Beerbohm.

Mr. Max Beerbohm, whose clever essays and caricatures, &c., have secured for him a position in the world of art and letters, writes a curious, but particularly characteristic, "hand."

Language (united names); Form (shapely, print-like capitals); Size (even margin maintained—letters equi-distant); Wit (rapid, wavy style); Constructiveness (original shape of letters); Imitation (easy mode of forming writing); and Ideality (delicate, light pen-strokes), which are amongst his largest intellectual

ADVANCED STUDIES

organs, show, according to their developments, the direction in which his genius lies. His judgment of configuration, dimensions, &c., is very good, and his Mirthfulness causes him to see things through a humorous medium. His imitation and constructive talent add the capacity to imitate, reproduce, and put together such ideas as are presented to his mind.

His Ideality gives him a love of finish in all he does. The writing is minute: it shows him to be exceedingly particular as regards the working out and completion of all he attempts. He does not dash off his work and think "that will do, it's good enough." No! he thinks, "how can I improve upon it, in what way can it be made more perfect?"

He has excellent power for putting pen to paper other than by drawing: he is a good writer.

He has a lively imagination, a whimsical fancy all his own. The wide curves to the letters show a "credencive" cast of mind. He is fond of novelty, and is ever ready to imbibe new ideas, and take in fresh information.

He takes an interest in whatever is *outré* or out-of-the-way. The plain matter-of-fact and prosaic will do for some people well enough, but not for him. He looks for something *bizarre*, and has an eye to the strange and unconventional.

The light, free touch denotes refinement of feeling, and a nature such as is opposed to grossness and coarseness.

Love of animals and children is revealed by the loops of the *x*, *b*, and *h*.

MRS. BERNARD-BEERE.

A common or uninteresting autograph this is not, revealing, as it does, its owner's marked individuality. The strokes of which it is constituted are—(1) decisive, and (2) without any absurd or extravagant movement. The signs of mental culture are visible, moreover, in the "Greek" forms of the letter *e*. The length, vigour, and ascendant motion of the strokes of which the letters are composed tell of activity, *verve*, and power of enthusiasm; which necessary qualities are well backed up by the energy, innate force, and determination which are signified by the thickness and bluntness of the lines which cross the *F*, and appear under the name, and also do duty for the hyphens between the names "Bernard" and "Beere."

Now, as regards the qualifications requisite for a great actress: in the separation of many of the letters, *B* from *e*, *n* from *a*, *r* from *d*, and so on, we have the sign for Human Nature—instinctive judgment of character; in the large, sweeping strokes of the *d* and *F* there are imaginative powers, which, in their turn, are supplemented by originality of mind, as shown by the uncommon form of the flourish—if indeed it can be called by that name—beneath the signature, among other things.

Add, to these intellectual powers, emulation or ambition (as manifested by the upward climb of the whole line of writing), and we obtain, as a *resultant*, many of the qualities which give dramatic aspirations and histrionic talent.

In this autograph, the large size of the letters generally shows self-respect and pride—aristocratic, or "proper" enough—but, all the same, *pride*. The presence of the line accentuates this dignity.

The *wave-like form* of this stroke, by the way, indicates a forcible, persistent, and, at the same time, strongly sensitive nature.

Mrs. Bernard-Beere, whilst being fond of hard work (and not merely so from the desire of winning its reward either, but rather from a positive affection for exertion), is also partial to the enjoyments of life, and will be fond of the pleasures of existence, of "all things bright and beautiful," as indicated by the thick, strong, and, withal, elegant style.

Power of determination is a prime element in this gifted lady's character, as well as the above factors.

Mrs. Annie Besant.

Mrs. Besant, the great high priestess of theosophy, an occult science which owes its revival chiefly to her and the late Madame H. P. Blavatsky, has the signs of spirituality (bases of letters widely curved), benevolence (sloping " hand," outstretched finals, &c.), and conscientiousness (level placing of letters) all prominently displayed in her handwriting, which shows her to be of an exceedingly impressionable and receptive psychical nature (which accounts for her interest in all occult studies), and possessed of great sympathy, a desire to benefit and befriend mankind, and extreme straightforwardness and honesty of motive. She is absorbed in the contemplation of the unseen, and is willing to believe in and to be convinced of what is termed the " marvellous," and will sacrifice much in order to investigate and demonstrate that which she believes and knows to be the truth. Her great feeling for others, her administrative gifts, and her faith and belief in humanity, have caused her to continue in welldoing, and to have ever before her the uplifting and ennobling of the race, although she is not unlikely to have been, at times, disappointed in those around her.

ADVANCED STUDIES

Her Firmness being only of moderate or average development (finals rather faint, non-rigid style), she is open to conviction—not obstinate, dogmatic, or unreasonable, though the high-barred *t* shows us the leader, the independent thinker. Bigotry, intolerance, or narrow-minded conventionality will not accord with this rather uncommon, curvilinear " hand." Her mind is eclectic; it is the storehouse for wisdom—Eastern and Western. Her selective talents, as well as her critical and reasoning faculties, are shown in the absence of *liaison* between the *s* and *a;* her ideality, in the refined style, as a whole. She is logical, keenly moved by all that is worthy of admiration, and contemplative. There is sufficient self-esteem in the tall capitals to render her dignified, though not egotistical. She hates bounce, self-advertisement, or bombast. The almost equal heights of the small letters proclaim her to be capable of giving her mind to one thing exclusively; hence her capacity to master the many complex subjects which she has studied, and her patient willingness to await results as a student thereof. She has a strong love of harmony and concord, and although she has good executive power (see the strokes under the names, and to the *t*), and will, therefore, take pleasure in disseminating the doctrines which she has undertaken to advocate, her destructiveness not being large (the lines being *thin*), she does not wish to *break down*, and would not wilfully kill even an insect. Brawls, tumults, and "scenes" —no matter whether or no they are occasioned in defence of a "good cause"—would be repugnant to her. Altruistic, philosophical, and highly nervous by nature, she will advance and promulgate the views which she feels will benefit others; is an optimist, and understands that evolution is carrying forward the progress of humanity—surely, if slowly.

We may learn much from this autograph, for Mrs. Besant herself is a highly-developed character—sincere, intellectual, and spiritual.

MRS. PATRICK CAMPBELL.

Mrs. Patrick Campbell has been described, and not inaptly described either, as a "bundle of nerves." The hasty, hurried movement of the handwriting proves the intense character of her temperament, and indicates further the mental activity and extreme sensibility with which she is endowed. Possessed of an excessively susceptible, impressionable disposition, Mrs. Campbell has shown us the scope of her art in such widely different plays as "The Second Mrs. Tanqueray," "Little Eyeolf," and "Pelleas and

Melisande," and thereby revealed, not only her highly emotional capacity, but her poetic feeling and high æsthetic tastes. Her predominant mental system is plainly shown in the rapidly turned-off "hand"; and this, associated as it is with large Language (names connected), Form (shapely capitals), and Ideality (well-curved style), and good Constructiveness (the commencements of S and C made to do duty for the crossings at the t's), account for much of her dramatic talent. Her Time and Tune are well defined, being indicated respectively in the outward curvature of the strokes and the even flow of the writing.

She is, therefore, musical; but the organs aid her, in conjunction with her language, in giving to her voice the peculiarly fascinating charm which those who have heard it will remember. She is fond of indulging in reveries, and will be capable of considering herself actually as the character she undertakes to personate. This testifies to her convincing method and her hold over her audience. Approbativeness is evinced in the upward canter of the signature, and this faculty will have the effect of making her sensitive to criticism, and apt to feel slights keenly. She has pet ambitions, and is gratified when they take a definite shape and are realised and appreciated. She will be highly agreeable, winsome, and taking in her manner, though, at the same time, not fond of general society (letters near together); she will be attached to children, however, or any pets she may possess (C

attached to *a* and *B* to *e* by means of loops). Such is Mrs. Campbell in outline.

In a recent number of a very popular monthly, a novelist, about whom much has been written, expressed it as her opinion that nobody upon the English stage was "worth seeing," and that acting, "if an art at all," was on "the lowest rung of the ladder." She further compared histrions to monkeys, and, by so doing, it must be added, displayed not merely a great want of discrimination, but a lamentable lack of knowledge of mental science. True, some actors, comedians, and "comic" players are imitative, but not so all. Tragedians are far more creative artists than many writers of to-day, and are also far more finished and artistic and original than many concocters of fiction. If people would but study phrenology, physiognomy, and graphology, silly assertions such as these (which betray ignorance and prejudice) would not emanate from their lips.

"CHEIRO."

Cheiro, who has earned an enviable reputation as the greatest male palmist of the day, writes a rather cramped-up, thick "hand," which leans in the "wrong" direction. The faculties which are in a high state of development, or activity, with him, are the Perceptive group, along with Comparison, Human Nature, Agreeableness, Wit, Imitation, Ideality, Sublimity, Caution, Marvellousness, Approbativeness, Force, Secretiveness, and Amativeness. The heavy appearance of the writing, and the shapely forms of the strokes, will make him appreciative of all kinds of pleasures— of all things that appeal to the senses, and which give enjoyment. He is fond of the beautiful—has a good memory for faces, and this, added to his innate intuitive conception of character, aids his palmisteric judgments.

As a rule (although itself certainly not the specific sign for the trait), this back-handed style is usually seen with persons who are interested in the occult and supernatural; *the* sign for "Belief," or "Wonder," love of and faith in the extraordinary and out-of-the-way matters, I have located in the *wide curving* of the bases of the letters (of the *C*, particularly in the case before us), and in the exaggerated "heads" of the letters—as, for example, in the large upper section of the *C*, and the inflated loop of the *h* and *C*.)

Cheiro's large Approbativeness (flourish below name) in conjunction with well-marked Secretiveness (letters narrow—restraint manifested in tracing down strokes), makes him capable of exercising a good deal of *finesse*, tact, and management with others; hence, in giving readings of character from the hand, he is able to put even disagreeable truths in such a way as not to wound the feelings of his clients. He has rather small Friendship, but large Agreeableness—as the huddled-up letters and wide curve of the *second* up-stroke of the *h* respectively show.

Thus, although he is not fond of society in general, he is not without the capacity for making himself very amiable and bland when in the company of those around him. He is timid, naturally—as the dot of the *i* shows, by being placed in the *rear* of that letter,—and very anxious to be thought well of, has not so good an opinion of himself as he desires other people to have of him,—and is rather apt to be dreamy and morbid.

His will, however, is strong (thick, blunt terminals), and he is not without energy or the power of bringing to pass what he wishes (line under name thick and long); and these facts will modify the more unpractical side of the character. Allied with those long up-and-down strokes, I generally find a great love of travel—and, as Cheiro is observant (upper part of "body" of *h* angular, among other signs), it may be assumed that he is fond of "seeing the world."

THE REV. JOHN CLIFFORD, M.A., D.D.

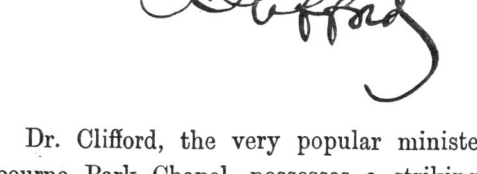

Dr. Clifford, the very popular minister of Westbourne Park Chapel, possesses a striking and fascinating personality, which is well disclosed by a careful perusal of his autograph, every line and stop of which tells of a distinct individuality.

Judged from an "outsider's" point of view, the signature (reproduced) is elegant, because constructed on a curvilinear plan; yet, although this gives us the *clue* to the reverend gentleman's character, it is only when we proceed to inspect the graphic signs *individually*, that we perceive the mental and moral worth of our subject.

Endowed with a high degree of the nervous temperament, as can be observed from the diminutive, "frisky-looking" pen-strokes (I know not how else to describe them), Dr. Clifford has all the "go," intensity, work-brittleness, and wide-awake nature that fit him to carry out the arduous duties of a clergyman.

That final to the *d* is an eccentric one. Lethargy and happiness are totally incompatible with Dr.

Clifford. He must be actively engaged—and this zeal, enthusiasm, and spirit of his, strike his hearers and all who come in contact with him—animate them and fire them with ardour—to accomplish something worthy of living in this world of ours.

His love of children, implied by the ample loops to *C*, *l*, and *d*, is one of his strongest social sentiments. In teaching the young, therefore, he would be in his right element, for those who have the happy gift of imparting instruction to the little ones are always highly appreciated by them — children invariably knowing who understand them best.

Spirituality (wide curves to the bases of the letters), Veneration (high position of dot above *i*), and Benevolence (flowing terminal to *d*), are amongst the most active organs of the moral group.

He is, therefore, exceedingly impressible, trustful in Providence, reverential, devout, and beneficent. He has a strong conviction in regard to the efficacy of a higher power, and is much influenced by his religious feelings.

Conscientiousness (even straightforward style) and Firmness (forcible pen-strokes) are both exceedingly influential; and though his Hope may not be quite so dominant—being modified somewhat by Caution (*i*-dot placed *over* the letter) and Secretiveness (*o* and *d* closed)—he is quite sanguine and confident.

The praise of God, rather than that of men, would be sought by Dr. Clifford. He is wishful to do the right thing, and would not merely act in accordance with the wishes of others in the hope of gaining their applause. He values, in fact, their *friendship* rather than their approbation; their *goodwill* rather than their acquiescence.

He wishes *to be* rather than to seem; and, however much he may appreciate a good name, position and reputation, merely as such, appeal to him very little.

Language is well indicated by the *liaison* of the *J* with the *C*: hence he has command of words, and, as a preacher, would be able to choose such as would convey his meaning adequately and precisely.

His judgment, discernment, clearness of mental vision, and capacity for deep thought are his strong points. Therefore, all he does is marked by judicious foresight and discrimination—he plans ahead, and has great facilities for arranging and combining his ideas. Practical above all things, Dr. Clifford does not believe in mere theories—in creeds or sectarianism. He understands perfectly that, though others may be working on different lines from himself, they are yet striving for the same results. Therefore he is content.

He is "matter-of-fact," but not devoid of poetry of feeling.

His Ideality is well represented in the symmetrical curves, and his Sublimity in the enlargement of the same. Time (regular flow of writing) and Tune (rounding out of sides of letters), moreover, are

186 THE LANGUAGE OF HANDWRITING

well enough developed to ensure Dr. Clifford's possessing a keen sense of melody; he appreciates music highly—no matter whether or no he actually professes to be an exponent of the art.

MR. FREDERIC H. COWEN.

In the handwriting no specific signs have hitherto been discovered as indicative of either Time or Tune, and musical ability has been deduced by graphologists, more particularly by observing the formation of the handwriting in its entirety, than by inspecting the letters in order to find the presence of any special graphic sign.

But Tune is a talent possessed by those in whom the muscular system is either dominant or, at least, well defined, as a rule; hence, as persons of this stamp are characterised by a curved conformation of body, the shape of the letters of their handwriting will be also in a like manner rounded, and this because the whole body, together with their movements, is constructed on a curvilineal principle.

Now, before us we have the signature of an eminent musician—that of the well-known composer, Mr. Frederic H. Cowen. How does the autograph bear out my theories? We will proceed to examine it, and find out. In the first place, in order that we may not jump at our conclusions, we will commence our investigations by observing the signs typical of the "textural indications"—*i.e.* the condition of the organism. It will be perceived that the strokes which comprise the various letters are direct, well-regulated, and non-complicated; in short, they are "simplicity itself"; hence the quality of the organisation is high. There is also culture, in combination with natural refinement, nicety of feeling and susceptibility, signified by the *tout-ensemble* of this elegant, harmonious, and delicate piece of penmanship.

Mr. Cowen, we thus learn, has a refined mind, and a favourably organised constitution; the mental and vital elements ranging higher than those of the motive system. There is evidently a good development of the perceptive group of faculties—notably of Form (symmetrical, print-like capitals), Size (equal, regular shape of letters), Colour (rather thick "down-strokes"), and Language (H connected to C of surname)—such being all needed by a musician. For instance, Form gives him the capacity to commit the notes to memory; Size the ability to judge of the fitness, adaptability, and proportion of one portion of a composition to another; and Colour the necessary sense of colour and warmth of expression; while Language lends fluency and power of utterance to his ideas.

Tune, as I have said, I determined upon according to the rotundity of the letters; nearly, if not absolutely all great composers exhibiting in their handwriting a continuous curve in the formations of their letters—the down or up-strokes being rarely of a rectilineal character. Here the peculiarity alluded to will be noticed.

Time, I find, is usually shown according to the regularity apparent in the handwriting—for the reason that the motion and mode of progression of those who have a clear conception of the laws of Time, are periodical — a soldier, for instance, having a fixed method of walking, his arms swinging like a pendulum at his side.

In the signature of Mr. Cowen the regularity of alignment, the even, harmonious movement of the writing, and the beautifully adjusted pen-strokes will at once strike the observer.

Order, giving attention to minutiæ and carefulness, as well as the love of arrangement, perfection, and neatness generally, combined with his large and full Ideality and Constructiveness—softly curved, symmetrical letters, H connected to C—is plainly denoted by the dot which is duly placed over the i, and also by the care bestowed upon the handwriting generally.

Comparison, which engenders lucidity of thought and critical faculty; Mirthfulness, which gives appreciation of humour, and Agreeableness, are all well above the average; these faculties being respectively typified by the clearness of the strokes; the waviness of the final, and the continuous downward curvature exhibited in forming the letters (*n*, for instance, being shaped like a *u*).

Other organs which are well developed in Mr. Cowen are: Benevolence—sloping, rounded "hand"; Spirituality—wide curves at bases of letters; Conscientiousness—letters very level; Approbativeness—flourish beneath signature; and Combativeness (which gives executive power, and is more defensive than aggressive in this case),—terminal trending to the left, &c.

The domestic and social sentiments are, naturally, well represented; and perhaps Friendship, Inhabitiveness, and Parental Love—which are shown: (1) by the wide spacing, (2) the looping of the letters, and (3) the stroke employed to unite the two up-strokes of the capital *H*—are as large of these groups as any.

MISS LOÏE FULLER.

Miss Loïe Fuller, whose autograph is given herewith, has, as can be seen by its inclined and somewhat irregular strokes, a keenly sensitive, impressible temperament.

The strong movement of the handwriting, which is its chief feature, shows great variability of mood; its (usually) large dimensions indicate impulse, and the (generally) thick F crossings, &c., denote vivacity, energy, and *verve*.

Amongst Miss Fuller's largest, or most active "organs," may be mentioned her Weight (consistent slant of letters), Form (symmetrical shapes of letters), Time (even flow of writing), and Constructiveness (original form of capitals, &c.), which materially assist her in dancing, giving her, as they do, a conception of the laws of gravity, motion, and marked individuality in all she attempts.

The *length* of the strokes is very remarkable, showing expertness, activity, both of mind and body.

There are dramatic talents revealed — a strong perception of humour is shown by the sharp tracing and wavy " head " of the F — imitative ability by the letters of various sizes, and suavity in the *u*-shaped *er*, &c., which give charm of manner, power of adapting herself to her surroundings, and elasticity of mind.

The almost perfect curves and light style signify refinement of mind : ideality being thereby represented. Hence, all she does is in good taste.

She is fond of receiving applause, moreover, as the rather flourishy capitals and embellishment below the same signify. Approbativeness aids her in a marked degree with what she does, and causes her to be desirous of winning the favour of others. Tact is shown in the diminution in the size of the letters towards the ends of the words.

Miss Fuller likes society; witness the wide spaces between the letters, and she does not at all relish the idea of being second to any in the affection of those she likes. Altogether, it may be said of La Loïe Fuller that she has, in every way, the requirements for taking, as she has, some foremost position in the world of entertaining; that she has a warm, affectionate nature, quick sympathies, a keen sense of humour, and a desire to take an active part in whatever sphere of life she may be placed.

MR. WILLIAM SCHWENCK GILBERT.

It has most truly been said that the capacity for taking "infinite pains" constitutes *Genius*, and Mr. W. S. Gilbert's autograph (reproduced herewith), if it proves nothing else, bears testimony to the assertion.

Everything about it shows—not merely cultivation and talent—but *carefulness*, deliberation, and thoroughness: there has been no undue hurrying over the process of forming the letters—which, whilst being uttered by a ready, quick motion of the hand, are all thoroughly legible and plainly delineated.

Mr. Gilbert's gifts are many, and of a varied description, as everybody knows. He is, at once, an excellent draughtsman and the most skilful humorous verse-writer we have.

His Form and Size—shown by the proportional and well-shaped letters—are largely responsible for his talent in the former direction; whilst his well-indicated Time, Language, Mirthfulness, and Ingenuity—shown by (a) the measured flow and (b) general connection of the letters, and (c) the "throw-off" of the (d) uncommon *G*—contribute towards his power in the latter.

Human-Nature (*G* separated from *i*) and Order (*i* dotted, methodical style) are both very well denoted; and our subject's Conscientiousness (letters evenly set down upon the paper in a row) and Firmness (*t* strongly barred and *G*'s terminal finished bluntly) both assist him in bringing forth the "fruit"—which readers of the inimitable "Bab Ballads" and such as revel in the "Gilbert-and-Sullivan" Savoy Operas enjoy so much.

There is more quiet dignity about this specimen than love of display. There is, truth to tell, very little showfulness implied. Discretion, reticence, and caution in acting are all well represented in the compression of the letters.

Mr. Gilbert has stated, in an interview, that he is

about as unmusical as any man can be—and it will be observed the down- and up-strokes of his signature do not round out.

Of course, it is unnecessary to enter into "negative" qualities; but, as the sense of "Rhythm"—of which nobody probably ever had a better development than Mr. Gilbert—has been confounded with "musical capacity," it is as well, in this particular case, to draw special attention to the above fact.

The truth is, that *Rhythm* is—as all phrenologists are aware—one of the functions of Time—and, as such, proves to be one of the leading factors in Mr. W. S. Gilbert's interesting personality.

DR. NEWMAN HALL.

In this autograph, that of the Rev. Newman Hall, the *directness* and *straightness* of the strokes arrest our attention before anything else. The moral nature is of a very high type, the intellectual also; neither is inferior in any way to the other. His temperament is about equally balanced, Firmness (steady style, terminal to *l* hooked); Conscientiousness (even, rectilinear type of writing); Veneration (unostentatious capitals); Hope (final of *n* raised); and Benevolence (extended finals, &c.), are all pre-eminent, and about as well defined as one another. These make Dr. Hall a true Christian, governed by the principles of justice, morality, and submissive to a higher power, and trustful in Providence, and above all, charitable. Approbativeness is not dominant here; therefore he is not led over much by the voice of the people. He is not "all things to all men," but has a quiet dignity, and strives to be *one* thing to his Maker. He must entertain very clear notions in regard to what is right and what is wrong. He cannot act or think in opposition to what his conscience tells him is the former. Nay, this assertion may be qualified by saying that he must further, as far as lies in his power, any cause which he considers right. He adheres to and advocates whatever he feels and knows is for the best. He is not easily swayed in his opinions, and is as consistent as a man can be; nor is he narrow-minded, nor anything but practical. That rather bold writing, with its constantly connected characters, was never yet seen to accompany "fads" in the writer. He gathers knowledge quickly, observes readily, and makes the best use of what he knows (angular, clear letters). His order is well marked, consequently he works methodically and lays out his plans after a set course. Routine and regularity characterise Dr.

Hall. To act without forethought—to speak without giving due reflection to his subject—would be utterly foreign to him.

His mind must be still very bright and clear, notwithstanding the fact that, in answering my request for his autograph, he reminds me that he is in his 82nd year. Care and prudence, deliberation, harmony, and sincerity are among Dr. Newman Hall's "strong points." The signs for Form (symmetrical shapes of letters) and Size (same placed at equal distances apart), give evidence of Dr. Hall's gift for water-colour sketching, which, according to *Who's Who*, is his hobby.

LORD GEORGE HAMILTON.

"To know when to sit still"

George Hamilton

Lord George Hamilton's handwriting, a specimen of which is herewith presented, shows, by the rapidly-delineated and somewhat irregularly-placed letters, mental activity, quickness of thought, and sensitiveness of organisation.

The clearness of the various strokes, considered with reference to their easy, but rather hurried-over, appearance, denotes lucidity of ideas; and the manner in which the letters decrease in size, become smaller and less distinct at the terminations of the words, shows perspicacity, tact, and the ability to keep his own counsel.

The high position of the dot over the *i* denotes reverence, also a conservative spirit, if judged in relation to the controlling force suggested by the well-regulated pen-movement of the whole handwriting, as shown in its compact formation.

Energy, which is directed, governed, and supplemented by firmness and discretion, is shown by the short, black bars which cross the *t* ; self-respect and dignity are shown by the fairly tall capitals ; and a good degree of friendliness and sociability is revealed by the rather wide intervals between the letters.

In the *u*-shaped *n* and *m*, as well as in the rather undulating stamp of handwriting—the line described by the march of the letters being somewhat irregular and serpentine—we perceive the indications of adaptability, diplomatic talent, and *savoir faire* ; and the loops, which are noticeable in many cases, indicate kindliness and the power of loving others.

In all respects this is a superior type of penmanship, and suggests such mental cultivation and will-power as we should expect Lord George Hamilton to possess.

It is not given to all who are in " the House " to be individually gifted; but Lord George Hamilton, it must be said, possesses a marked personality ; one quite *his own*; and hence plays an important part in British politics, not merely on account of his high social positon, but also because of his initiatory will-power and all-round ability.

THE REV. HUGH REGINALD HAWEIS.

To answer the question as to wherein lies the great strength of the Rev. H. R. Haweis, who has attained eminence not only as a preacher, but as a lecturer, author, journalist, critic, and musician into the bargain, were no easy task, for so many gifts are necessarily possessed by him that the combination is such as to perplex any but the practised student of human nature. Nevertheless, graphology comes to our aid, and it is by its means that we will dissect our subject's composition.

Mr. Haweis then has, to begin with, a predominant mental temperament. This is shown by the irregular nervous, spirited, erratic signature of his, which is subjoined. Added to this, amongst his largest organs are undoubtedly his Language (letters mostly connected), Constructiveness (*H* and *R* formed in an original manner, and so that the one would be incomplete without the other), Tune (curvilinear shapes of most letters—observe *w, e,* and *i* especially), Comparison (distinct method of tracing letters—note the *e* is cleanly cut, without a blind loop), and, indeed, the intellectual faculties generally.

The way in which the above are displayed serves to account for Mr. Haweis's musical and dramatic talent, his eloquence, "style," critical acumen, and interest in whatever is going forward. He does not believe in dissociating religion and human nature. There is great independence in those tall capitals. The extreme High or Low Church, therefore, would never suit his ideas of what religion ought to be. He believes in liberty—and, I am bound to say, cares very little for the notions of those who hold bigoted or intolerant views. He wants to hear "all sides." That large handwriting deals with wide principles and generalities.

There is the sign of Locality in the length of the strokes generally, whereby we get the *raison d'être* of Mr. Haweis's love of travel. The letters are formed of wide curves at their bases—this implies a receptive cast of mind. They are of unequal heights; and this fact tells of Mr. Haweis's versatility of mind. In his books or in his sermons he is never dull, he always has something fresh to communicate, and says it in an attractive, unconventional manner.

There is Wit in the rapid pen-tracing—which assures us of the source of his humour; his quaint way of delivering an address or lecture. Some object to the excitation of mirthfulness in church, but, provided it is not exercised at the expense of Veneration, there is no reason whatever why it should not be called into play. It is a God-given faculty; and I have heard from the lips of Spiritualists that the departed are just as full of fun in the other world as they were here. Mr. Haweis's discrimination, his ability to take in a wide field of ideas, and to deal with complex subjects, are some of his strongest points, and hence he is known, and rightly so, as a Broad Churchman. No doubt it is in a great degree due to Mr. Haweis's magnetic personality that he is able to hold his hearers so well; and it will be observed that the handwriting is somewhat black, as is mostly the case with that of those who exert much influence in the world.

There is no lack of social feeling in the wide intervals between the letters, and a great deal of energy is exhibited in the vigorous method of forming the same, and in the well-barred H.

This autograph is full of character, and it would be easy to enlarge upon what has already been said, but that is unnecessary, Though we are tempted to go further into Mr. Haweis's character, space forbids our doing so, therefore the rest of the weighty graphical signs which we have reluctantly been obliged to leave unnoticed I commend to the student's patience and judgment to solve, by the rules already given in the previous studies.

Mr. John Page Hopps.

Mr. Hopps possesses a favourably-balanced temperament, the mental elements predominating.

His writing is of a distinctly "literary" type—small, indicating great attentiveness to detail, with the names connected, telling of command of language. The perceptive faculties are large. Form (shapely capitals), Individuality (bases of letters angular), and Colour (strokes alternately thick and thin) especially. He has excellent judgment and reasoning power, much capacity to manipulate minutiæ, and great ability to deal with matters of fact, the critical faculties being strong. Although our subject is interested in and has written ably upon Spiritualism, in an admirable little work entitled "Death a Delusion," which may be accounted for by his active spirituality (wide curves to bases of *o* and *s*, &c.), he is too practical and sensible to be led by superstitious notions, and we may well accept whatever he has investigated as being the truth. His love of all that is so is indicated by the letters being set in a straight line. He hates imposition, lying, and hypocrisy, and will maintain all that is just, equable, and honest.

The blunt terminals (to the p's especially) tell of average or full firmness. Mr. Hopps, therefore, has decision, and, although he is ready to alter his opinions if he feels they are wrong, he could not well be without some sort of purpose in view and fixity of principle. Generosity is shown in the out-stretched terminal of the s. He is, therefore, charitable, and able to make full allowances for others, capable of sympathising with them and of making their trials his own.

There is little conventionality in this free and easy style, with its (relatively) tall capitals; certainly nothing superficial or indicative of "pose." The development of Time, which is shown by the quick, even movement of the writing, may well be associated with the mind out of which "Pilgrim Songs" sprang, and there is the gravity in the final of the s, which we might easily connect with the pathos of these poems. He has a healthy organisation, however, and is not morbid, though imaginative, as can be seen, and energetic (well-marked lines of signature).

He is affectionate (well-sloped style), not particularly fond of society with a big S (letters close together), and has very strong feelings; is fond of animals and children, and very intuitive in his instincts (*P* separated from *a*).

THE REV. FATHER IGNATIUS, O.S.B.

Ignatius, O.S.B
Monk

This is an extraordinary autograph, the handwriting of an uncommon man.

Prominently displayed are the signs for his large Veneration (*i*-dot placed high), Firmness (rigid style—angular—and finals blunt), Language (*o* and *s* united), Tune (up- and down-strokes curvated), and Comparison (clearly-traced " hand," loops to *g* and *o* not blotted), which, considered in relation to his marked Executiveness (mounting writing, *t* well crossed, bar *descendant*, *i* well dotted), show us the outlines of the character for which he has become famous.

Possessed of a strongly devotional spirit, great fixity of purpose, tenacity, eloquence, musical gifts, critical faculties of a high order, and untiring energy, Father Ignatius has proved that where the will and affection are, there will be the way also.

The capitals are rather large, and the bases of the

letters mostly broad. He has self-assurance, also belief in the power which guides his actions and thoughts, and this will have the effect of composing his mind. It endows him with a quiet self-possession, a calm tranquillity, which, to be understood, must be realised.

Observe the stops after the word " Ignatius, *O. S. B.*" They tell of order, of forethought, of attention to small matters (as they are called). The writing is not very large. Who can mistake its indications? Nothing escapes our subject, no detail is overlooked, no matter, even of minor importance, is thought too insignificant for full consideration. His insight and power of discrimination are unique. There is lucidity and precision there; there is the capacity for taking infinite trouble; and there is sincerity. Father Ignatius will be spent very gladly on behalf of the life-work which he undertakes; he will not do his duties carelessly; he will not abuse his charge.

Imagination is not lacking. Notice the exaggerated ending to the *k*, among other signs. The dark strokes, too, tell of *magnetism*, of power over his hearers. It is this quality which, in addition to his clear, forcible eloquence, carries so much conviction with it over his hearers' minds.

He is ecstatical, and throws his whole soul into whatever he does. Herein lies the secret of his success, for his genius as a preacher, musician, and writer is undoubted.

Mr. Henry Arthur Jones.

Through the courtesy of Mr. Henry Arthur Jones, the celebrated dramatist, I am able to give the accompanying autograph, which, as we shall see when we come to examine it, forms a very typical and interesting example.

Henry Arthur Jones

The sharp, shortly-turned pen-strokes which compose this signature signify a predominance of the mental system, which gives intellectual power, activity of mind, and a relatively large brain.

That the organic quality is high, it is needless to add, since the pen movement which produces the strokes that constitute the various individual letters, is just—and only just—sufficient in order to allow of the letters assuming their shapes at all. Not an inch, nor a quarter of an inch, too much nerve-force has been expended in their formation. The faculties which are the most prominent in this specimen are, amongst others, Language (y connected to A with a continuous stroke), Form (elegant, shapely capitals), Individuality (acute bases to letters), Size (well-proportioned and equidistant letters, two strokes of *H* parallel), Causality (*J* separated from *o*, &c.), Comparison (clear, unconfused pen-strokes, *J* not united with *o*), Human Nature (regular spaces between letters), Ideality (neat and delicate strokes to all the letters), and Constructiveness (original forms of capitals), which, taken together, give him power of thought, originality of ideas, a strong sense of perfection and the fitness of things, as well as attention to detail, thoroughness in work, and penetrating insight. His power of observation, instinctive judgment of character, and fluency of ideas (combined with power of verbal expression) are among his best-defined intellectual attributes.

In addition to a finely organised mind and strong dramatic instincts, Mr. Jones's Conscientiousness (letters running in a level line), Firmness (decisive, firm, and blunt strokes), Hope (upward tendency of writing), and Executiveness (forward movement of letters, *t* barred with an advancing line of moderate thickness) endow him with a painstaking, energetic, and fairly sanguine temperament. The length of the capital letters—of the *J* especially—tells of Activity. Our subject must be doing something: he never lets the "grass grow under his feet."

His Energy and Ambition (forcible and upward march of handwriting) are, however, fairly well checked by his Caution and Prudence (careful, temperate strokes and rather low letters).

There is no "happy-go-lucky" inclination exhibited,

206 THE LANGUAGE OF HANDWRITING

neither does Mr. Jones spend his time in "building castles in the air;" and the way in which the energy is directed and expended will be well considered for the most part.

In the slant of the letters to the right we have the sign for sensibility and kindness of heart, whilst from the rather wide spaces between each of them, we notice that there must be a fair degree of the faculty of Friendship—which together give Mr. Jones wide interests.

There is not any excessive Self-esteem shown by this autograph, but the Independence (t barred rather high), power of resolution, and unconventionality of character, signified by the writing as a whole, will be remarked by all who have studied written gesture, even though they may have had no previous knowledge of the science of Graphology.

THE REV. W. J. KNOX-LITTLE.

Canon of Worcester.

[signature: W. J. Knox Little]

In presenting the signature of the Rev. Canon Knox-Little, who is one of the finest preachers in the

Church of England, I can only say that we have before us one more striking proof of the truth of Graphology.

As may be anticipated, the organic quality of this eminent cleric's "make-up" is high—as is shown by the efficacious, yet not redundant, pen-strokes; whilst the fervour and "tension" of his whole nature—due to a strong and active mental system—are amply borne out in the sharp, brisk movement of the writing, the very dots and stops being angular. Of course, it goes without saying that the intellectual, or frontal lobes of the brain are in a high state of development; but the moral regions are also equally influential.

Of the former it may be noticed that Language (names, "Knox" and "Little," united), Order (stops placed after W, J, and at the end of the signature), Form (simple, almost print-like forms of capital letters), Individuality (strokes all distinct and sharply defined), and Comparison (clear handwriting, &c.), are strongly denoted.

Human Nature is also large—as the broken x, among other things, shows; in the rest of the handwriting it is even more conspicuous.

Of all the moral organs, according to his handwriting, Veneration is by far the most active—if not absolutely the largest—as may be seen by the very great height at which the dot above the i flies over that letter; and this faculty gives elevation of mind, respect for greatness, aspiration, a sense of holiness, and reverence. It is owing to the prominence of this organ, in a great degree, that Canon Knox-Little is a High Churchman. Very well defined, too, are his Conscientiousness (letters level), Firmness (blunt terminations to strokes), Hope (final turned up), and Benevolence (sloping style, terminals thrown out), which make him stable in his views, true to his convictions, a believer in the future state and in the hereafter, and, withal, charitable and sympathetic—as all true clergymen should be.

After these organs, how strongly, we may observe, are Destructiveness (thick crossing to *t*, and black bar under names), Combativeness (lines long and advancing), and Dignity (tall capitals, *t* crossed high) indicated; and these faculties give untiring energy, force of character, moral and physical courage, and vigour in all things undertaken—whether in speaking, writing, or what not.

By no means deficient, either, are the Domestic attributes—as the slope, looping, and thickness of the strokes all indicate; still, these hardly appear to be called into play as are the rest of his faculties. From the tendency shown to huddle many of the letters together, and the thoughtfulness exhibited in the handwriting, it is probable that Canon Knox-Little is not averse from being "alone with his thoughts," sometimes, and that he does not hanker after society.

Taking the outlines of Canon Knox - Little's

character, it may be said that he possesses an intensely ardent, strongly susceptible organism, his feelings and sensations being extremely warm and vivid—hence his impassioned style.

I have chosen Canon Knox-Little's signature—which he was kind enough to allow to be reproduced for this purpose—in order to show the combination of qualities present in a *religious* and *clever* man.

An utterly mistaken, unfounded idea appears to be prevalent nowadays, that if a person be the former he or she is, as a matter of course, not the latter, and *vice versâ*. That this notion is entirely erroneous I have been at some pains to prove in this book; and were a selection of the most famous—*truly great*—people to be made, it would be seen at once that such was not the case.

As regards *Religion*—it is a complex word, and, of course, a more complex subject.

Comparatively few people have no religion — though many a person's "faith" is unconventional, and free of all sects and creeds. In respect to *clergymen*, I say no more than that, although we cannot expect *perfection* in *them*, yet we *do* expect, and *ought to have*, the very best men for the ministry obtainable, it being, if rightly maintained, one of the most honourable of callings, no matter whether the form of belief be Protestantism, Romanism, Lutheranism, or anything else.

Mr. Andrew Lang.

Mr. Andrew Lang's calligraphy—for such in reality it is to the student of graphology—is, like most authors', small, rapidly traced, and endowed with a sprightly eccentricity which individualises it, and stamps it as *his own*. Of course, the short, yet ample strokes, which are never extravagant or redundant, proclaim superiority in respect to quality of organisation, and so on; but it is only when we come to inspect the writing closely that we perceive the marked talents of the writer set forth by it.

The remarks which are about to be made should be prefaced by stating that, in the present case, the letters of which the sign manual is composed are mostly united (as can be seen), whereas in the rest of the writing in the note which Mr. Lang has been kind enough to place for my consideration—which, he assures me, is his " normal hand "—they mostly stand apart. This is directly the opposite state of affairs to that which was remarked upon in connection with the study that constituted a critique of Mr. Wilson Barrett's " style."

In what way, it may be asked, are our " subject's " abilities manifested by his handwriting? This is the all-important point for discussion; hence let us commence our graphological survey. Language: *A* connected with *L;* Constructiveness: method of uniting the one with the other, original; Ideality: flowing stroke connecting the two capitals; Causality and Comparison: *L* separated from *ang*, combine to give him freedom and originality of expression as well as artistic instincts, perception, and love of refinement, beauty, and the abstract and metaphysical it may be. From the writing of the body of the letter one is led to believe that Mr. Lang is, by nature, or partly by circumstances, fond of theory and ideas *as such*—of the ideal and philosophical—but the signature, which is subjoined, gives the *practical* instincts which are so necessary in this world.

The small size of the writing denotes love of detail —of working out one's schemes according to system; and the stop placed after the surname indicates orderly habits in regard to work—a painstaking, thorough, careful mind.

The height of the capital letters shows a good degree of Self-Esteem, which begets self-reliance and confidence. There is nothing "swagger" about this autograph; therefore there is not much showfulness or love of admiration. As a whole, the graphologist would pronounce the writer of this "hand," whoever he or she might be, to be possessed of marked abilities, literary talents, great continuity of purpose, and economical in his or her methods; also sharp-sighted and prudent. Though perhaps reserved—companionable with those whom he (or she) liked—capable of thinking and doing while others might be only *talking*.

There is one special graphical sign to which I should like to direct my readers' attention before concluding this short analysis—it is the direction of the sweeping stroke which crosses the *A*. It will be seen that it trends, with a circular movement, to the left before advancing to the right. This tells, up to a certain point, of a protective spirit—so say some authorities; but I have usually found this kind of loop associated with large love of home or country. Hence I believe it to be the graphological equivalent for Inhabitiveness—love of place. To some extent the sweep of the stroke, it will be noticed, is defensive, since it tends from right to left; but "protective" instincts may spring from various sources—the term is indefinite. Wide observation will confirm, or it may be overthrow, my reading of the graphical sign.

Miss Evelyn Millard.

It is a great pleasure to present, and a still greater to delineate, the character which is indicated by the autograph of Miss Evelyn Millard, whose position in the dramatic world is almost unique.

ADVANCED STUDIES

She has a strong predominance of the nervous—often called the mental—temperament, which is shown by the short, sharp, animated strokes of which the handwriting is composed.

The slight inequality in the height of the letters shows acute mental sensibility, and a keenly sensitive, highly-strung, excitably-organised nature.

There is a rapidity of movement shown in this specimen which results in producing a certain sharpness in the outlines and contours of the letters—as, for example, in the terminations of the *E* and *d*—hence there is a naturally impulsive, ardent, enthusiastic disposition signified.

The great *artistic* capacity of Miss Millard is revealed by, among other things, the *curved* pen-movements which have traced the letters. She has æsthetic tastes, a highly-original mind, and an altogether superior type of intellect.

The *quickness* of the handwriting, or rather its animated appearance, indicates a quick-witted, active-minded temperament.

The faculties which are indicated in the highest degree are:—Language (names connected by flowing stroke), Colour (bases of letters thick), Human Nature [1] (*E* set standing alone, and other letters equidistant), Sublimity (rather large sweeps to

---

[1] This faculty has been brought into play, naturally, by our subject; hence it is shown better in the *rest* of the autograph, it indicating the activity of the organs.

strokes which terminate *E* and *d*), and Ideality (very finished and chaste forms of letters), which, taken together, make her ready of speech, a good elocutionist, vivid in her methods, refined in style, and "true to nature" in her portrayal of character.

To these organs we may add Weight—shown by the usually consistent slant of the letters—which gives her grace in walking and ease in deportment, and Constructiveness—denoted by the unusual shape of the *E*—which makes her skilful and unconventional in her manner of presenting the *rôles* she undertakes.

Large Form (well-controlled strokes of which capitals are composed) and Size (letters generally at equal distances from each other) aid her materially in keeping in view before her the whole characters portrayed, as well as helping her in deciding upon appropriate gestures with which to invest them, while Mirthfulness (quickly-turned, wavy strokes to many of the letters) assists in comedy scenes and those of a light vein.

There is a good deal of mental order indicated, which is the outcome of her active Ideality, to a great extent; therefore, Miss Millard is a great lover of perfection and finish: ordinary, matter-of-fact details —trivial fussiness—may bother her, but she does not care for things "in the rough." She is clear in her ideas, although not provokingly precise.

Her Conscientiousness, which is larger than her

Love of Praise, is well indicated by the *evenness* of the straightforwardly-turned strokes and their relative consistency, and this, with her Critical faculty, causes her to be only too ready to see any possible errors in her "readings" when acting. She is, consequently, painstaking—more, however, from the love of being so than from any mere desire for applause.

This is a distinctly high type of handwriting in every way, and I would ask my readers to observe how simple and "homely" are the shapes of the letters, which, while denoting fine abilities, indicate an unusual absence of all Self-Assertion, and Humility. Miss Millard is *not* very self-confident, but then no truly great artists ever are.

A large amount of Energy and Force of Mind, which arise from fine developments of Executiveness and Firmness, give her thoroughness and a painstaking, determined character, the signs of these faculties being the thick, blunt horizontal strokes of the *E* and *d*.

In short, it may be said (and that without exaggeration) that the combination of qualities indicated by this particularly interesting specimen, as can be seen, gives excellent dramatic abilities and creative talents, besides poetic instincts. The imagination, impressibility, and emotional capacity of the whole organism are such as adapt their possessor for the exacting demands of histrionism, although literary talents as well are shown, and the whole character is such as could succeed in many branches of art beside that followed.

THE REV. ALFRED WILLIAMS MOMERIE,
M.A., D.Sc., LL.D.

The Rev. Dr. Momerie's writing, a specimen of which is given herewith, is particularly characteristic. The strokes have been traced with a quick, non-complicated pen-movement, which tells of his predominant mental temperament. The quality of Dr. Momerie's organisation is particularly high, as the fine, delicate tracing indicates; and the whole aspect of the writing reveals a nature such as derives far more enjoyment from contemplating the intellectual and psychological phases of life, than engaging in the pursuit of sensual, "worldly" pleasure. The *curve* is very much in evidence in the formation of the letters. Here we get a clue as to Dr. Momerie's intellectual bias. He has large Causality (*f* and *r*, and *M* and *o* apart) and Comparison (clear, unconfused writing), Human Nature, Wit, Imitation, Ideality, and Sublimity being likewise shown by the usual signs—the equidistant, readily turned-out, supple, elegant, and sweeping forms of the letters.

To the action of these organs may be attributed his lucid powers of reason, his logical capacity, and his gift for following up a train of argument; also his insight into the human soul, his discriminating talent, and his love of all that is beautiful, sublime, and poetical. His Language (names connected) affords him the gift for imparting his knowledge with facility. It gives him the requisite command of words by means of which to convey his meaning, whether in writing or otherwise. As a speaker, he comes under the head of the "Electric" class. The moral group is exceedingly active and influential. Spirituality (wide bases to letters) is strongly indicated, and this makes Dr. Momerie inclined to dwell upon the unseen world. This faculty, working with his Causality, &c., disposes him to trace, so far as may be possible, the origin of the higher nature of mankind. It makes him interested in their spiritual attributes, and causes him to pursue philosophy and metaphysics. He may or may not be aware of the fact, but he is gifted with the spirit of prophecy—he has presentiments, or will, generally speaking, be correct if he attempt to forecast what is about to happen. Things frequently turn out just as he anticipates. He has great insight and inspiration. He loves justice, and mercy, and temperance, and is not by nature a pessimist—for the writing is even, inclined, and very delicate, and the signature ascends. But so sensitive and idealistic a temperament is doomed to suffer keen disappointment. Dr. Momerie has a nature such as is easily approached (letters far apart), and his sympathy is unbounded—he knows no nice distinctions of party, sect, or creed; he has a wonderfully expansive, comprehensive cast of mind, and can take in much that would offend more narrow people. He understands well enough how much nearer perfection some people are than others, but he gravitates towards the pure and the good, and his feelings for the fallen are true and strong. He has high aspirations, and believes that mankind may develop high possibilities; is frank, sincere, and very unconventional—though the high-dotted *i* gives evidence of a high degree of Veneration and respect for all that is noble and good.

SIR LEWIS MORRIS.

He writes a somewhat small, nervous-looking "hand," which proceeds from a sharply-delineated pen-movement. The strokes are definite, to the purpose, and just adequate; hence the organic quality is high. On this account there is a superior cast of brain, exquisiteness of feeling and organisation, and strong susceptibility. The size of the letters themselves being small, rather than large, and their appearance being sharp and yet fairly fluent, we may decide upon there being a strong predominance of the mental or nervous system.

The fluency of style, and the rapidity of utterance in expressing the letters, tell of large Language and power of words, which faculty, acting with a fine degree of Ideality, Comparison, and Construction (shown respectively by the delicacy, symmetry, originality, and clearness of the lines which constitute the letters), as it is in this case, gives many of the "poetic" attributes. Thus, Sir Lewis is refined, capable of experiencing elevation of thought and feeling, able to see the beauty of imagery and symbolism, and the fantastical in art and nature, as well as to draw similes, discover analogies, &c.

The faculty of Time, which, in order to be a good poet, a person must needs have largely represented, in order that he or she may appreciate and comprehend the laws of rhythm, &c., is indicated by the regularity of the movement of the writing, principally.

Spirituality, which gives an interest in the supernatural, the love of musing upon, and, to some extent, belief in, the unseen and intangible, is denoted by the rather wide curves of the letters at their bases. The light, aerial stamp of writing, and also the large capital *L*, show an imaginative and non-materialistic temperament.

The wavy stroke beneath the signature shows an appreciation of humour, as well as the love of being thought well of and of receiving approbation.

In summing up this character, we may briefly state that Sir Lewis Morris has a finely constituted organism, high mental powers, and an essentially artistic and literary bent of mind. He is fond of indulging in reverie, but when he comes to commit his ideas to paper, can work out his imaginings in detail (small "hand"). He has an idealistic, critical type of intellect; but, at the same time, is not wanting in either feeling, kindliness, or sympathy, as his inclined, curved, and well spaced-out style shows.

Miss Alma Murray.

Below is given the signature of Miss Alma Murray (Mrs. Forman), who is so well known both in the capacity of an actress and a reciter, that no words of introduction are necessary.

Alma Murray Forman

In the autograph the delicacy and grace of the strokes arrest our attention before anything else. Refinement of mind, sensitiveness of feeling, and susceptibility of organisation are prominent features;

ADVANCED STUDIES

therefore, Miss Alma Murray's mental temperament predominates, and that in a striking degree.

There is no materialism shown, and the animal nature is absent; comparatively speaking, that is to say; for, of course, there is a normal development of the feelings and sentiments.

In the sharpness of the strokes, and the rather unequal method of placing a few of them here and there, as well as in the slightly irregular movement of the writing, as a whole, we have the sign for nervous excitability, which tends to make our subject extremely impressible; indisposed to take things easily; and intense, as, indeed, all good actresses should be and are.

There is considerable activity of nature revealed, and love of physical exercise, by the long stroke to the y in "Murray." As a whole, the intellectual region of the brain is well developed; the excellently-represented perceptive group, in which Individuality is indicated by the acuteness with which some of the letters are imbued; Weight by the letters sloping mostly in one direction; and Size by the even margin and well-adjusted letters generally, will make Miss Murray penetrating and observant; while the clearness of the handwriting, in addition, will cause her to be definite, and the reverse of "scatter-brained" in her impressions.

Although, in the signature, the good development of the organ of Language which she possesses is not especially well shown, in the rest of the handwriting which Miss Alma Murray has been kind enough to place at my disposal for this study of her personality, it is revealed by the tendency frequently exhibited to connect the words to one another.

In Miss Murray's dramatic creations, her vivid intelligence, grasp of character, conscientiousness and thoroughness of treatment are always apparent; these essential qualities being indicated in her handwriting by the legibility of, and the regular spaces between, the letters, and the evenness of their setting.

There is evidence of a strong imagination—Ideality being well defined in the harmonious types of most of the letters, but it is well governed; while Firmness, Executiveness, and Force, shown respectively by the blunt final strokes, the black bar across the letter F, and the thick horizontal lines, add power of determination, energy, and "backbone."

Though somewhat ambitious and desirous for success, Miss Alma Murray lacks in a great degree self-confidence; she is apt to become solicitous and timid. I would give her, too, more Hope (the finals descend mostly); however, she has a very fair degree of Secretiveness (as readers of this study can see for themselves if they glance at the closed vowels, &c.), and without this all-important faculty, few actors ever become famous, as it gives them the power for concealing their own personalities, and sinking and cloaking, as it were, their feelings for the time being.

Having touched upon the more patent characteristics

ADVANCED STUDIES

of this autograph, in summing up, it may be said that our subject is a lady possessed of much mental and physical activity, elevation of feeling, and decision of purpose; she is distinctly versatile, sensitive, and imaginative, being acute in her judgment of human nature, motives, and character.

Her ardour and artistic feelings give her the inclination to turn the talents she possesses to practical account.

There is a great deal of capacity for taking trouble indicated, moreover; whilst a forcible personality, and a lack of vanity, are also well defined attributes.

MISS NETHERSOLE.

This signature, as any student of graphology will observe, is a very artistic specimen of handwriting.

The *curvation* of the strokes is very marked, and the requisite fine *Quality* of organisation is indicated by the delicate " pen-touch " upon the paper.

As a whole, Miss Nethersole's autograph shows great emotional capacity, and a very highly-wrought, exquisitely-constituted organism, with a predominant mental temperament.

Large Sublimity (large size of letters), Ideality (elegant, graceful style), and Language (capitals united with the small letters following them, &c.), as well as Constructiveness (*t* bar cleverly connected to *s*, eccentric forms of capitals), and Intuition (*a* detached, and *r* and *s* separated), are amongst our subject's best-developed faculties; and these combine to give her a vivid imagination, dramatic talent, intensity of method, and an inclination to follow her own bent, rather than the "beaten track."

The executive ability, which adds *force* to all she attempts, is seen in a marked degree—in the *three separate* lines under the names; and hence we have the *raison d'être* of her *tragic* power.

Miss Nethersole will throw her "whole soul" earnestly into all she does, and go about her work "with a will." She would be, obviously, much influenced and impressed—according to the type of character she was personating.

She aims very high indeed (ascendant style), and must be desirous of taking rank with the best actresses of the day.

Ardent, enthusiastic, sensitive, tender-hearted, and highly-strung—such is Miss Nethersole—according to her ascending, sloping, and soft-looking handwriting.

MAX O'RELL.

The specimen of handwriting reproduced herewith will be recognised by our readers as the autograph of Max O'Rell, the witty author of "John Bull and his Island."

Among M. Blouët's largest intellectual developments are his Eventuality and Individuality (small size of letters, attention to detail, diæresis over *e*, &c.), Comparison (clear style), Causality (*P* separated from *aul*), Mirthfulness (readily turned-out style), and Human Nature (letters at equal distances apart, in addition to other signs).

The high mentality disclosed by the signs for these faculties, added to our subject's culture (shown by the cultivated pen-tracing exhibited in the forms of the letters), accounts for Max O'Rell's literary talents, since it inclines him to be observant, keen to perceive and reason, critical in his judgment, intuitive, and practical. He sees not only the defects of things, but also their excellence; can detect the imperfections, and discern the good points in literature, art, &c., very readily; is logical, moreover, and disposed to think out his plans.

Language is denoted by the connected names. Therefore, he must be capable of proving himself to be not only an amusing entertainer, but a most diverting companion in his home circle as well.

He is not slow to see a joke; takes in a ludicrous situation with a keen relish; is much "tickled" with the incongruity of things which he sometimes sees, and is naturally humorous, playful, and endowed with a strong sense of the ridiculous.

Although he is progressive, energetic, and self-reliant, judging from the thick line below the names and the relatively tall capitals, he is also cautious and prudent. Observe the shortened terminals, also the two small marks directly over the *e*. He does not, therefore, trust "to chance," or to "appearances"; looks somewhat ahead, and, with his large Firmness and full Continuity (shown respectively by the thick, heavy, steady lines under the name, and to the *t*, &c., and the even style), is enabled, by giving his mind to what he is about, to achieve most things that he attempts.

His Self-Esteem aids him much. It enables him to form his opinions independently, to act irrespective of others, if he thinks by so doing he is acting consistently, and to dare to do what he would otherwise fear to commence, much less carry through.

Though there is discretion in the carefully closed-up *a*, *o*, and *u*, there is no indication of anything like hypocrisy. All the letters run straight ahead, onward

—they do not take a circuitous course upon the paper.

Courageous, bold, intense, conscientious, beholden to no man, active, eager, yet capable of running no risk if he can help it; matter-of-fact, and, at the same time, possessed of no little originality, or imagination, and talents of a pronounced description—such, in short, is Max O'Rell, whose character, as denoted by his handwriting, once more proves the utility and value of graphology.

Mr. George William Erskine Russell.

The subject of this sketch will be recognised by most of my readers as a brilliant litterateur, an ex-M.P., and the President of the Liberal Churchmen's Union.

His temperament is mental, with an adeqate development of both the vital and motive systems—as is shown by the rapidly-traced and sharply-turned-off, yet, at the same time, somewhat rotund and certainly vigorous, pen-strokes. Hence he may be said to be "well-balanced" as regards these conditions, for he is capable of fulfilling his duties, of carrying out his projects, and of withstanding the obstacles created by circumstances or the drawbacks of surroundings. Having the pleasure of sitting just in front of Mr. Russell recently, I was much struck by his full, bright eyes—the signs of his active centres for language. This faculty is so well shown in the handwriting, too, that the letters, *in the signature*— not in the rest of the specimen from which the autograph is taken, be it noted—are all *united*, which fact accounts for many of the graphical signs so well indicated in the writing in the body of the letter being literally "crowded out" in the sign-manual.

Mr. Russell is artistic as well as literary. In proof of this assertion witness the beautifully curvated style—the *G* and *R* particularly. He has, moreover, keen powers of discrimination, and much taste, refinement, and delicacy of perception.

Tune, as indicated by the full, outward curvation of the up- and down-strokes, proclaims Mr. Russell to be musical by nature. He may not be a composer, or even an executant; but he will be fond of concord, appreciate harmony, and—as a natural consequence —abhor discord.

That mount of the handwriting, especially as it is accompanied by the little impatient curly line under the names, means *enthusiasm*.

These strokes are not tortuous. They get "to the

front," for which they are destined, without delay; like their writer, they mean "business," "BUSINESS," "BUSINESS."

The slope of the writing to the right shows large benevolence. Mr. Russell is not a hard, cold, unsympathetic, unresponsive, "standstill" man. He is no dreamy theorist; no halting, half-hearted individual.

His feelings are ever with the oppressed and downtrodden, and his executive faculties prompt him to aid them. This was shown in his help on behalf of the Greeks some little while ago.

Mr. Russell is not readily "hoodwinked," is very clear-headed, and fond of all that is high, noble, elevating, and deserving of admiration and respect.

Whilst being ambitious (upward slant of writing) he does not wish to play up to people.

What he believes is in a person retaining and developing his or her own peculiar "personality"—whatever that may be. He would be disgusted with anything like the "humility" dodge of the unprincipled, or indignant with those who would cringe, crawl, or creep along life's road.

Liberty and progress, enterprise and volition, are all remarkably characteristic of our subject, whose autograph, it must be admitted, is not the *least* interesting of those which we have had the privilege of studying.

Miss Marie Tempest.

One more musical type of handwriting is embodied in the autograph of Miss Marie Tempest, which is given herewith in *facsimile*. In this specimen the strokes are (1) curved, (2) dark, (3) slightly sloping, and (4) possessed of breadth rather than length. These facts tell of a predominance of the vital temperament. The signs of mental culture and education are numerous in this signature. The letters are, for instance, traced readily and without effort; they are also of graceful, yet somewhat unconventional, forms; whilst the Greek-shaped *e*'s, and the second up-stroke of the letter *p* being separated from the down-strokes in "Tempest," corroborate and extend these indications of intellectual cultivation. The up-strokes of the letters being longer than their tails, and the strokes which cross the *t* and underline the signature being at the same time thick, as though a considerable amount of pressure had been expended upon them, I consider that mental activity rather than bodily exercise would find most favour with Miss Tempest, and also that her energies are directed to and employed more in mental than physical channels. In any case all who have heard her sing will acknowledge most assuredly that Miss Marie Tempest throws her whole soul into her work, and does it with a hearty good will—her "might," as has been said.

How thoroughly well trained her vocalisation is, moreover, all who understand and appreciate good music will know. Now, respecting the indications of our subject's musical talents, what are they in the handwriting? Well, according to my own notion, they are exhibited in the wide outward curves, which compose the letters a and e, &c. Could we give a larger sample of Miss Tempest's handwriting, it would be seen that her autograph was one mass of curves linked together. Tune having been duly taken, Time calls for our attention in the next place. It is indicated by the continuous and even flow of the handwriting. The pen appears to be well under the control of the operator; hence there is a certain harmony in the whole character of the letters. My reasons for assigning the faculty of Time to this graphological sign were given in my analysis of Mr. Cowen's autograph. Artistic tastes are plainly shown in this autograph before us. Form and Ideality, giving a great love of the beautiful, are shown in the symmetrical shapes of the capitals, and the finish of the writing; while Colour, giving perception of effect in the arrangement of colour, &c., and Order, giving capacity for neatness and precision, are well indicated, judging from the thickness of the commencement of the head of the letter *e*, and the presence of the dots above the *i*, and at the end of the name.

The form of the *T* is remarkably simple, yet, from that very fact, by no means commonplace. The serpentine form of the cross-bar over it, and of the stroke which begins the *M*, shows a strong fund of humour and vivacity. The small *m* is so formed that it appears inverted; this is the sign for suavity and adaptableness. Miss Marie Tempest, therefore, ought to be excellent company, for, in addition to her accomplishments, she is capable of making herself very amiable and pleasant, although, from the closed *a*, and the tendency exhibited to make the letters smaller at the ends of the words, I do not think she would let everybody into her secrets. She has plenty of tact, but is independent and self-willed (bar to *T* flying above the stroke it is intended to cross), possessed of much self-respect—or, as some term it, "proper pride" —is fond of liberty and freedom, besides being quite able to push herself forward to the front (lines to *t*'s, and under signature advancing) without assistance, and is desirous of holding a foremost position in the world (writing slightly ascendant, first ascension of *M* taller than the second, and slight tendency to run to flourish).

With this spirit, versatility, innate shrewdness, and personal fascination, added to her beautiful vocal gifts, is it strange that Miss Marie Tempest has taken a leading position in the ranks of the musical-dramatic world?

Mr. Hermann Vezin.

[signature: Hermann Vezin, Jan 5./97.]

Perhaps, throughout the whole series of autographs comprised in this volume, there is none as obviously characteristic as the one which we are now about to consider.

Grace, elegance, and refinement are apparent in its cultivated outlines; poetic feeling of no mean order being suggested by the well-nigh perfect curves of, for instance, the *V* and *z*.

Precision of form is shown in these symmetrical capital letters; and the faculties of Language (*H* looped on to *e*), Size (letters equidistant), Order (*i* dotted, stop placed after names), Human Nature (*V* separated from *e*, and *m* from *a* likewise), Comparison (letters clear—strokes never muddled), and Ideality (beautiful sweeps to loop of *H* and upstroke of *V*) all aid dramatic art, whether our subject be instructing others or acting himself.

There is some evidence of "Weight" in the parallelism of the strokes, which, together with Tune—out-curving letters—and Time—regular flow of the same—assist in pitching the voice, and give tone, accent, cadence, and so forth, to Mr. Vezin's utterances.

There is love of harmony and sympathy shown by the even, well-sloped letters; no little elevation of feeling, in the light, delicate style; and power of concentration in the pretty well equal height of the letters.

There is ambition in the ascending letters; not a little executive ability in the "throw-off" of the V; and a degree of conscientiousness, shown by the letters being placed regularly in a line, that would give stability and thoroughness to all undertaken and carried out.

The form of the loop such as is to be seen in the H one generally finds allied with strong paternal instincts; hence, Mr. Vezin ought to be fond of children; he has tact, according to the "dwindling away" of the letters at the ends of the names, moreover, and this, with the restraint shown by the closed-up a, should give him not only reserve power, but also capacity for managing and carrying out his plans.

Sir Samuel Wilks, Bart., M.D.

Our study, which is a particularly interesting one, is that of the late President of the Royal College of Physicians, Sir Samuel Wilks, Bart., M.D., F.R.S. His handwriting indicates a predominance of the mental-nervous system, from the fact of its being small, sharp, and lively, or animated in appearance.

The fine quality of the organisation is indicated by the absence of all complication or confusion of the strokes of which it is composed.

If we proceed to inspect the character of the writing carefully, we shall notice that the *straight line* and *angle* are more in evidence than the *curve*—indicating *scientific* and *practical* (as opposed to *artistic*) powers.

As a whole, the reflective faculties are very highly developed; and thus (the powers of observation being, also, well indicated) there will be a natural love of inquiry, of investigation, and reasoning, both *a posteriori* and *a priori*.

All the small letters in the signature are united, and the capitals not connected thereto, the letters being acute and very tiny.

There is a great love of acquiring knowledge shown —acquisitiveness being indicated by the short upstroke with which the *W* commences, and large order (*i* duly dotted) will add (if considered in relation to the critical powers of our subject) a great notion of method, arrangement in ideas, and love of neatness and care in all things undertaken. Sir Samuel has decidedly large Form, Size, and Weight also, and these organs assist him in his professional duties.

He has very well-marked Individuality and Human Nature, shown by the small size and angular shapes of the letters, and the even distances and absence of connecting strokes between some of them. All good medical men possess the penetrating insight engendered by these all-important faculties.

Other organs which appear to be large and influential are: Caution (dot of *i* placed directly *over* the letter, among other signs), Continuity (letters small and of equal heights, &c.), and Conscientiousness (letters level and regular), with a balanced degree of Secretiveness (*a* closed—signs of restraint visible in handwriting), which give Sir Samuel a prudent nature, application of mind, thoroughness, and judicious reserve.

In reviewing this personality, one's attention is arrested by the subject's (1) capacity for detail, (2) his clearness of intellect, and (3) power for understanding complex ideas, which result in producing the superior mentality Sir Samuel Wilks possesses. This small, carefully-traced, easily formed, and somewhat angular writing impresses us at first sight.

To do justice to its numerous indications would be an utter impossibility; but enough has already been said for all practical purposes.

Scientists deserve our deepest regard, for they are intent upon solving the problems of Nature—her truths; and it must be borne in mind that to do this, though only in part, demands first, integrity, and secondly, comprehensiveness of intellect.

Madame Hilda Wilson.

The wide, full-bodied letters, the contours of which are curved, announce the predominance of the vital elements in this celebrated vocalist's constitution.

Her musical talents are shown in the following manner:—(1) Melody, by the rounding out of the letters, and (2) Time, by their continuous flow and measured utterance, so to speak. Language, shown by the united names, adds power of expression; and it is noteworthy that all good musicians—no matter whether they be executants or composers—have this faculty in a high state of development. (See, for example, the autograph of Mr. Cowen, given on a preceding page.)

In Madame Wilson's signature there is impressionability in the inclination of the strokes; as well as a well-defined "colour-sense," which contributes force and power to her efforts (shown by the thickness of the lines).

As a whole, the Domestic group of faculties is remarkably well defined—witness, in proof of the assertion, the looping and wide spacing of the letters —and this, in conjunction with the warmth and ardour displayed by other signs (notice the ascendant final of the *W*, for example), gives Madame Wilson the power of enlisting the sympathies of her hearers, and carrying their feelings " away " with her singing.

The large dimensions of the letters assure us that there is more attention paid to things *as a whole* than *individually*. There is a tendency shown to exaggerate—to take extended views of matters and magnify.

The looped *d* suggests, not only mental cultivation, but imagination : whilst, in the flourish from the final *n*, we have typified power of assertion—the capacity for making herself heard in the world, and of fighting her way forward to the front.

XIII.

ADDITIONAL STUDIES

Sir Dyce Duckworth.

This signature is indicative of great activity, the signs for Executiveness (pronounced pen-movement) and Combativeness (ascending bar to *t* strongly defined) being very well shown. The mental manifestations are marked, especially the signs for Individuality (angularity of many of the letters), Order (dot placed after the signature), Comparison (some letters connected, and others separated), and Human Nature (many of the letters apart, and some of angular formations); while Self-esteem (tall capitals, &c.), Caution (terminals shortened), and Approbativeness (ascending handwriting) are all three well-defined traits.

THE LATE SIR JAMES PAGET.

The salient features of this autograph are great sensitiveness and feeling, which are indicated by the inclined and delicate strokes which constitute it. Two of the chief signs are those for Conscientiousness (perfectly even lines, the letters touching the same ground-floor) and Dignity (high capitals), which tell us that Sir James Paget is almost honour itself, and would never be guilty of stooping to do a dirty trick. The mental powers are equally well marked; the brain is active and the mind well regulated. The small dimensions of the individual letters give evidence of the mind that pays great attention to comparatively small matters; the *g* is not joined either to the *a* or the *e* which precede and follow it, and this, considered with reference to the rather pointed style, and the *extreme* clearness of the penmanship, gives us the critical, investigating, vigilant, and lucid mental bias peculiar to the successful medical man.

ADDITIONAL STUDIES

The late Sir Richard Quain.

The sign-manual here reproduced of Sir Richard Quain indicates much perspicacity and power of *finesse* by its "dwindled" strokes which do duty for the letters which terminate the names. The style is a somewhat curved and sloping one; hence we may infer that our subject has a full endowment of the *savoir faire*, or tact. The brain is a very active one in this case, and the mental energy (vigorous, hasty pen-movement) hardly permits the pen to form the individual letters. The signs for Form (elegant capitals), Order (small writing, dot placed over i), and refinement of mind (freedom of pen-movement, elegant cultured style) are all conspicuous; and those for Self-esteem (tall capitals, R spread out at its base), Executiveness (angular dot above i, ascending, pushing writing), Benevolence (wide curves), and Firmness (decisive, firm pen-strokes), are hardly secondary indications.

Sir Henry Thompson.

The letters which go towards composing the autograph of Sir Henry Thompson are angular, quickly traced, and sharply defined; thus indicating an active, penetrating mind, and a clear intelligence. The powers of Comparison (some letters connected and others separated) are strongly represented; the perceptive and reflective, or reasoning faculties, being both in a high state of development. Energy and Force are each of them leading features, as the ascending letters of the signature and lengthened terminal illustrate; whilst the blackness of the strokes accentuates these indications.

The Right Honourable Arthur James Balfour.

This autograph indicates that the reflective powers are highly developed; the mind being clear and the reasoning ability excellent (according to the clearness and the connection of the letters). The curious attachment of the capital *J* to the letters of the Christian name, where the stroke is first employed as a cross-bar to the *t*, shows that Constructiveness is well developed. The signs for Conscientiousness, Benevolence, and Self-esteem are all represented and indicated by the evenness of the letters at their bases, the wide spacing, and the tall capitals.

THE LATE ARCHBISHOP OF CANTERBURY (DR. BENSON).

His Grace's signature indicates considerable energy and executiveness by its mounting and decided strokes. The attention to detail is strongly manifested by the minuteness of the letters, and the colons which are placed after each word. The height of the capitals gives the sense of supremacy and self-reliance, which are so necessary in such a position; and the gliding motion of the *C* is said to denote the spirit of protection—which, it must be admitted, is a befitting characteristic for an archbishop. The signs for Firmness (some letters of angular formations, &c.) and Hope (final thrown upward) are strikingly displayed, as are also those for Ideality (capitals very curved, some letters separated, strokes of many of the letters somewhat irregular), Sublimity (large capitals), and Human Nature (strokes of many of the letters angular, many of the letters separated).

CARDINAL VAUGHAN.

The autograph of his Eminence the Archbishop of Westminster indicates prominently the signs for Constructiveness (d cleverly united to the V), Form (elegant capitals), and Language (flowing handwriting); whilst those for Benevolence (curved, well-parted letters), Hope (buoyant pen-movement), and Conscientiousness (letters of much the same size) are quite as apparent. There is a great amount of veneration, executiveness, and energy displayed by the "movement" of the letters, and the length of the final stroke; whilst the inherent affection and social attributes manifested by the somewhat dark, curved, and sloping handwriting, cannot be doubted.

LORD KITCHENER OF KHARTOUM.

Kitchener of Khartoum

This autograph is composed of a series of rigid pen-strokes, which show the strict disciplinarian. The close aspect of the writing, its carefully finished letters, their connection and restraint, point to reserve power; at the same time there is ardour and courage in the diagonally-placed and somewhat thick t bars. Intuition, in the absence of the connecting stroke between the t and c, in "Kitchener," is well marked.

The sense of duty (letters evenly arranged), of honour (names underlined), and personal dignity (tall capitals, high crossed t) is strong.

THE LANGUAGE OF HANDWRITING

THE LATE LORD RUSSELL OF KILLOWEN

[signature]

The handwriting of the late Lord Chief-Justice shows us the signs for his eloquence ("of" joined to "Killowen"), precision of thought and system (square-set style), and strong sympathy (in the right-handed slant of the strokes). The way in which the word *of* is connected to the *K* shows constructive capacity.

There is ambition in the upward march of the writing; dignity in the tall capitals and l's, and conscientiousness in the even placing of the letters. Altogether, a very characteristic autograph.

HIRAM S. MAXIM.

[signature]

This autograph, which is bounded by the straight line, shows practical interests, inasmuch as the letters are mostly connected. There is not much imagination shown, but order, in the well-attended-to stops, in combination with good judgment and the capacity for comprehending the application of principles, added to the clearness of thought manifested in the clean-cut strokes, and the sense of sublimity indicated by the large size of the letters, denotes the secret of his success.

DR. W. G. GRACE.

"W. G.'s" signature has been traced with an expansive pen-movement, showing a sanguine temperament—hence, love of out-door pursuits. Weight (consistently-sloped letters), Size (same equidistant) and Constructiveness (original and graceful forms of *g*) aid him as a cricketer, and good intellectual capacity is shown by the clear, cultivated writing, in which the *a* stands apart from the rest of the letters. Confidence in himself is betrayed in the height of the capitals; and consciousness of success in the flourish under the names.

"General" Booth.

The upright movement of this signature shows Self-dependence, which, in combination with "General" Booth's Language (connected names), Combativeness, and Destructiveness (thick, black line under signature), has assisted his efforts as a "muscular Christian." The tall capitals show Self-esteem, and the constrained appearance of the signature indicates that Deliberation, Forethought, and Shrewdness are not lacking. Practicability is shown by the connection of the small letters, and Acquisitiveness by the inward curve at the commencement of the *W*.

XIV.

HEALTH AND HANDWRITING

THE manifestation of mental power is, to a great extent, dependent upon the vigour or otherwise of the physical body. Of course, many intellectual people have a feeble frame, but that is no argument that but for it they would not have possessed their mental qualifications. All physical disability prevents a person making the fullest use of his faculties.

The movements of feeble people are uncertain and faltering; hence, broadly speaking, we shall find their handwriting lacking in force,—spiritless and lifeless. Want of vitality will cause the writing to droop,—the final strokes will descend, and we shall detect a want of ardour, freedom, and buoyancy.

Pulmonary trouble is often indicated by a superfluity of stops; cardiac mischief, by doubling of the down-stroke; whilst sterility has been said to be shown by the lack of *liaison* between the letters in the words.

But most people are aware that handwriting is expressive of the state of the writer's physical condition. Who is it does not recognise the shakiness of the pen-tracing of the aged or the dissipated? If the hand trembles when the state of the nerves is impaired, naturally the writing does so too.

AMELIA DYER.

Amelia Dyer

The autograph of the notorious murderer, Amelia Dyer, who, in 1896, drowned a number of young children near Reading, is formed of a series of hard, inflexible strokes. A brutal, heartless disposition is signified by its upright movement, considered in relation to the thickness of the lines. Notice the short finals and the close aspect of the signature. Her motive in committing her atrocities was *gain*. A total want of rectitude (unevenly-placed letters) aided her in what she did.

In "Mad Humanity" Dr. Forbes Winslow has a good deal to say with regard to the handwriting of the insane. He recognises perfectly the importance of written gesture as a means whereby we may obtain knowledge respecting the condition of persons mentally afflicted.

HEALTH AND HANDWRITING 251

Religious mania is indicated, as a rule, we find, by abnormal forms of the capital letters, especially *M*, *K*, *V*, and *W*. We can further notice the great height at which the *i*-dot soars, also the manner in which the terminals are carried up, in cases of the kind.

An example of insanity is seen in the annexed specimen :—

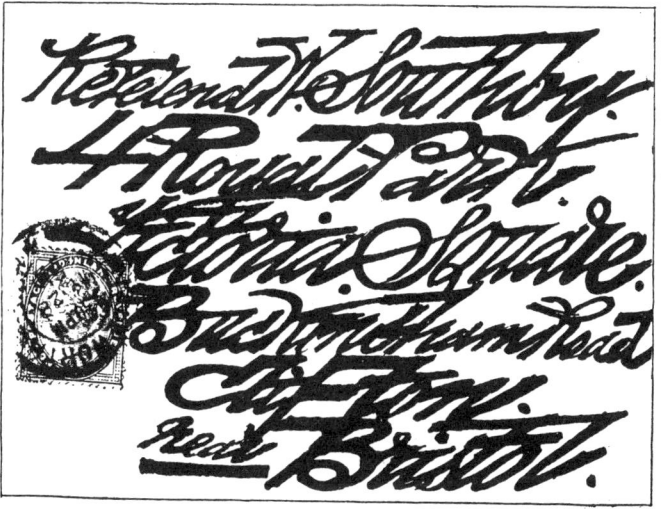

Observe the *Eccentric* style. Notice the utterly ungoverned appearance of the pen-movement, due to the extravagant expenditure of nerve-force. Of course all insanity is produced through the intense activity of particular brain-organs, and in this case the subject would be likely to manifest not a little self-will, and even "method in his madness."

The next sample of writing which is presented in this section is that of a person addicted to dipsomania.

In this case, the subject has excellent mental capacities, as the "nervous" style shows us. But, inspecting the pen-strokes closely, we notice a tremulous motion in conjunction with a swollen-out appearance of many of them. Of course, it does not follow that in every instance of intemperance we shall come across the same degree of tremor which is so conspicuous in this example, but, generally speaking, this peculiar jagging of the strokes is the accompaniment of voluptuousness in some one direction—opium-drugging, tippling, or excessive erotomania, it may be.

HEALTH AND HANDWRITING

As a specimen of handwriting indicative of excellent all-round physical vigour, I subjoin the autograph of a well-known tight-rope walker.

Here the steady, fairly heavy and very well-controlled strokes bespeak a good constitution, recuperative power, and a wiry organisation. If we remark the length of the y's tail we cannot fail to perceive our subject's athletic skill and agility—it being one of the principal graphical signs of muscular power.

XV

HANDWRITING AND HEREDITY

As examples of heredity in handwriting, the autograph of the Right Hon. Joseph Chamberlain, M.P., and that of his son, Mr. Austen Chamberlain, M.P., and those of Sir Henry, Mr. H. B., and Mr. Lawrence Irving are included. These are left to speak for themselves, to tell their own story. Naturally, they

J. Chamberlain

Austen Chamberlain

will show similar characteristics *where such actually exist* (or have existed), in the writers' characters; but, except as the sign-manuals of celebrities, they possess no special value, inasmuch as, were one anxious to investigate this branch of our subject, the *maternal*, as well as the *paternal* (to say nothing of the preceding generations') autographs would have to be studied.

One very deeply absorbing point is to notice (as I have often done) what features (facial) are alike in the cases of parent and offspring, and then what letters and graphic signs bear a resemblance to one another in such cases. It is strange, but certainly not extraordinary (if Graphology and Physiognomy are of any practical worth), that this parent's upper lip (say) is

long, and his capital letters are tall, as well as his child's.

There is an immense future before Graphology, as there is before all other cognate sciences. We are not yet in a position—and, I trust, never shall be in one—to sit down with folded hands and say we have discovered all that there is to be discovered. As long as human nature exists—as long as it remains what it is—"Human Nature"—so long will there be much left undiscovered about it.

Without doubt, other faculties, besides those already discovered, will be evolved. As the human race goes *onward* it goes *upward*. It is no use for theologians to lament because their creeds fail to convince; it is useless now trying to chain down people—nationally as well as individually—to this or that "persuasion." They will have none of it. This is essentially an age of *examination*—an age desirous of getting at the truth of things, whatever else it may be.

When, however, in its ignorance, it accepts the earthly as *absolute*—then a gross mistake is made. When it attributes *mind* to *matter*—instead of matter to mind—it unquestionably errs.

But, as it is only a "little knowledge" that leads to "atheism" (so called, rightly or wrongly), we may hope that the inquiring spirit of to-day may lead to the perfect establishment of the *divine truth*, as enunciated—not by the misinformed priests of the Middle Ages, nor of this or that sect even to-day, but by the Word of God—the Book of Nature—revealed and occult.

It may seem strange to the reader of this volume to treat so seriously what he or she esteems but as a frivolous amusement. Well, if the remarks just made seem to be out of place, they can be "skipped," or left unread. But, to the writer, no subject is so sacred, nor so *serious,* as the one with which Graphology deals.

To be able to read—though only in part—our fellow creatures; to be capable of understanding, of sympathising with them; of knowing how it is they fail; of helping them, by a word spoken in due season—is no little advantage, so, surely, no light affair.

BIBLIOGRAPHY

BALDO.—" A Method of Ascertaining the Habits and Qualities of a Writer by means of his Written Letters."
BARTER, JOHN.—" How to tell Character from Handwriting." London, N.D.
BAUGHAN, ROSA.—" Character Indicated by Handwriting." London, N.D.
BENNETT, WENTWORTH.—" A Dictionary of Handwriting and Character." London, 1896.
BLANE, JAMES.—" The Secrets of Graphology." London.
BYERLEY, THOS.—" Characteristic Signatures." 1823.
CELLA, EL SEÑOR DR.—*Flores Divinas de ciromancia.*
DELESTRE, M. J. B.—*De la Physiognomie.*
DESBAROLLES, A.—*Révélations Complêtes.* Paris (3eme Ed., 1895).
DESBAROLLES ET JEAN HIPPOLYTE.—*Mystères de l'ecriture* (2eme Ed., 1884).
FRITH, HENRY.—" A Guide to the Study of Graphology "; " How to Read Character in Handwriting." London, 1891.
GALIMATIA, SIEUR DE.—*Chiromancie Devoilée.*
GORRIE, EUGENE.—" Character and Handwriting." London, N.D.
HENZE, Herr.—" Chirogrammatomancy."
KEENE, J. HARRINGTON.—" The Mystery of Handwriting." Boston, 1896.
LAVATER, J. CASPAR.—" Physiognomical Fragments."

BIBLIOGRAPHY

LEE, DR. JOHN.—"Treatyse offe Chyrographye: wythe an artefulle and most pleasante wanderynge ine thee delectable maze of chyromancye."

LUMLEY, ED.—"Handwriting and Style."

MICHON, L'ABBÉ.—"The History of Napoleon I., determined from his Handwriting"; *Graphologie* (Journal issued 1873–1881); "A Memoir upon the Faulty Methods used by Experts in Handwriting"; "A Method of Graphologic Study"; "The History of Handwriting;" "System of Graphology"; "A Dictionary of the Notabilities of France judged from the Handwriting"; "The Handwriting of the French People since the Merovingian Epoch."

SCHOOLING, J. HOLT.—"Handwriting and Expression" (from the 3rd French edition of "L'écriture et le caractère," par J. Crepieux Jamin. Paris). London, 1892.

SCOT, MICHAEL.—"Hande Boke of Autographye."

STOCKER, R. D.—"A Concordance of Graphology and Physiognomy." London, 1896.

WHITE, Mrs. JOHN.—"How to Read Character from Handwriting." London.

THE END

Printed by BALLANTYNE, HANSON & CO.
Edinburgh & London